L-DOPA AND BEHAVIOR

L-DOPA
AND
BEHAVIOR

WITHDRAWN

EDITED BY

SIDNEY MALITZ, M.D.

Chief of Psychiatric Research
New York State Psychiatric Institute
New York City

RAVEN PRESS, PUBLISHERS ■ NEW YORK

Made in the United States of America

International Standard Book Number 0–911216–22–7
Library of Congress Catalog Card Number 75–181306

Contents

CONTENTS

List of Contributors

ANDRÉ BARBEAU, M.D.
Director, Department of Neurobiology, Clinical Research Institute of Montreal, Montreal, Canada

OTTO BENKERT, M.D.
Max-Planck Institute for Psychiatry, Munich, Germany

WILLIAM E. BUNNEY, JR., M.D.
Chief, Section on Psychiatry, Laboratory of Clinical Science, National Institute of Mental Health, Bethesda, Maryland

JOSEPH T. COYLE, M.D.
Johns Hopkins School of Medicine, Baltimore, Maryland

BRUCE DIAMOND, M.D.
Research Division, Central Islip State Hospital, Central Islip, New York

ROGER C. DUVOISIN, M.D.
Department of Neurology, College of Physicians & Surgeons of Columbia University, New York City, New York

GUY M. EVERETT, PH.D.
Department of Pharmacology, University of California Medical School, San Francisco, California

FREDERICK K. GOODWIN, M.D.
National Institutes of Health, Bethesda, Maryland

ALAN S. HORN, M.D.
Johns Hopkins School of Medicine, Baltimore, Maryland

MAUREEN KANZLER, M.D.
New York State Psychiatric Institute, New York City, New York

LIST OF CONTRIBUTORS

IRWIN J. KOPIN, M.D.
Chief, Laboratory of Clinical Science, National Institute of Mental Health, Bethesda, Maryland

SIDNEY MALITZ, M.D.
Chief of Psychiatric Research, New York State Psychiatric Institute, New York City, New York

N. MATUSSEK, M.D.
Max-Planck Institute for Psychiatry, Munich, Germany

SIDNEY MERLIS, M.D.
Director of Psychiatric Research, Central Islip State Hospital, Central Islip, New York

DENNIS L. MURPHY, M.D.
National Institutes of Health, Bethesda, Maryland

SOLOMON H. SNYDER, M.D.
Department of Pharmacology, Johns Hopkins University School of Medicine, Baltimore, Maryland

KENNETH M. TAYLOR, M.D.
Department of Pharmacology, Johns Hopkins University School of Medicine, Baltimore, Maryland

MELVIN D. YAHR, M.D.
Associate Dean, College of Physicians & Surgeons of Columbia University, and Director, Clinical Center for Research in Parkinson's and Allied Diseases, Department of Neurology, College of Physicians & Surgeons of Columbia University, New York City, New York

JOSE YARYURA-TOBIAS, M.D.
Research Division, Central Islip State Hospital, Central Islip, New York

Dopamine and Mental Function

André Barbeau

The biochemistry of mental disorders has been the subject of a great many reports, symposia, and monographs. Lately the field of cerebral monoamines has received increased attention, first with the "serotonin hypothesis" of Brodie,[21] then the "noradrenaline hypothesis" of Schildkraut.[68] In this chapter I will review the evidence indicating that yet another substance, dopamine, may have an important role in this respect. Dopamine, the direct precursor of noradrenaline, has a specific distribution pattern within the brain:[17] it is concentrated mainly within the striatum and substantia nigra. It is deficient in Parkinson's disease,[4,40] and this deficiency can be corrected with resultant sustained improvement in the clinical symptoms.[8] The motor functions of dopamine within the basal ganglia have been thoroughly reviewed by Hornykiewicz,[47] and we recently had occasion to survey the role of dopamine[14] and of the striatum[12] in autonomic and endocrine modulation. The use of L-dihydroxyphenylalanine (L-DOPA) in Parkinson's disease and in other disease entities[10] has been accompanied by a number of side-effects, many in the mental and psychological spheres.[13] Elucidation of the mechanisms underlying such effects may lead to the understanding of some aspects of mental disease. I will attempt to show in this chapter that in many instances dopamine is an important step in the postulated mechanisms and that the striatum plays a major role in the modulation of the autonomic, hormonal, and cortico-subcortical components of mental function.

CLINICAL EXPERIENCE

Depression

Since the early studies of Everett and Toman[42] and the subsequent ones of Brodie and collaborators,[21] many authors have been impressed by the interrelated biochemical changes occasionally found in severe depression.[60] For example, reserpine produces this syndrome in man after chronic use[54] and is known to deplete the animal brain of most amines.[21,27] An important part of the reserpine-induced syndrome, in both man and experimental animals, can be reversed by the administration of the precursor L-DOPA.[27,36] These observations have led Schildkraut[68] to postulate that severe endogenous depressions are due to a deficiency of amines, in particular of noradrenaline, at certain sites in the brain. The actual demonstration of such a deficiency has not yet been satisfactorily made, except indirectly in some patients who have committed suicide.[3] Thus it is still difficult to involve specifically any one of the best studied monoamines, i.e., noradrenaline, serotonin, and dopamine. In favor of the general hypothesis, we can, however, marshall the following evidence.

(1) Some drug-induced depressions, as mentioned above, have been reversed with L-DOPA. It must be

noted that in endogenous depressions low doses of L-DOPA were generally found to be ineffective.[51,61] With higher doses, occasional successes have been documented,[23-25] although the present evidence, as reviewed in other chapters of this volume, is inconclusive.[30]

(2) There is an apparent reversal of the state of depression (at least the "reactive" component) in most, but not all, parkinsonian patients treated with L-DOPA.[8] Actually, the only result which appears certain, besides the brightened outlook owing to improvement in overall functional capacities, is a definite degree of activation, the so-called "alerting effect." In addition, as I will try to demonstrate further in this chapter, there is also a definite improvement in the "set" (or preparedness) component of motor function.

(3) Therapeutic results are obtained with the monoamine oxidase inhibitors (MAOI) and the tricyclic antidepressants.[33] The MAOI are known to decrease the rate of metabolism of monoamines, whereas the tricyclic drugs are generally thought to interfere with cellular binding mechanisms. Further thoughts on this subject are expressed by Snyder and collaborators in this volume.

(4) Observation has been made of comparatively low amine or metabolite levels in the brain and cerebrospinal fluid of suicide victims.[3,37,69]

The evidence for the deficiency hypothesis is strong, but it is difficult to decide which of the individual amines is principally involved. The early studies implicated serotonin, and this is still a possibility; later evidence tended to favor a role for noradrenaline in mood regulation. This again is still a possibility. Now the L-DOPA data would appear to involve dopamine also, since it is generally accepted that most of the exogenously administered L-DOPA is transformed into dopamine within the brain. In total homogenates of brain, less than 1% of labeled L-DOPA is found as noradrenaline, and little increase in the tissue content of this amine can be measured.[26,44] However, regional studies indicate that L-DOPA may actually decrease the tissue content of noradrenaline in the hypothalamus and brainstem, probably through an increased rate of turnover in these regions.[29]

The complexity of the problem, as reflected by the conflicting biochemical data, is probably made worse by our loose definition of the term "depression." The study of parkinsonian patients treated with L-DOPA has greatly contributed to our understanding, and delineation, of the complementary signs of akinesia and rigidity. Indeed, in these patients we generally note increased vigor, a feeling of well-being, increased interest in the surroundings, increased freedom and spontaneity of movements, a greater willingness to partake in environmental activities, a desire to engage in conversation, a heightened wit, and improvement in recent memory, facial expressiveness, and mental concentration. Not until we applied a battery of objective tests[35,38] could any one of the behavioral signs be assigned to the symptoms rigidity or akinesia. We now know that akinesia is the first and only specific symptom to respond to L-DOPA therapy, and the only one to be correlated with a previous dopamine deficiency.[7,8] Applying the same clinical dissection, we would propose the following analysis of "depression" as generally defined.

In this syndrome of depression, it is possible to separate two major components: mood changes and motor retardation. The first symptom, mood, is a labile entity resulting from the precarious balance between alertness and the appreciation of the emotional content of the situation. Physiologically it again involves a balance between the states of activity of the ascending, reticular activating pathways and the limbic-hypothalamic pathways. In both these systems, the state of activity is modulated by competing noradrenergic and serotoninergic influences within an integrated network of interneurons. Mood is the psychic-emotional state resulting from the dynamic balance between the neurohormones in each system and the balance between the reticular and limbic-hypothalamic systems. Thus in our view, *both* serotonin and noradrenaline are involved in the genesis of mood; the apparent incongruity of clinical results with precursor amino acids or with inhibitors of amine metabolism is probably due to the fact that we look, in error, to the whole brain. Regional effects are obviously much more important. For example, a decreased serotonin metabolism in the limbic or hypothalamic system may be equivalent to hyperactivity in brainstem noradrenaline. It is even probable that the integration of the actual state of balance between neurotransmitters in each system is dependent upon modulation by higher centers (we have elsewhere postulated that the striatum plays the important role in this function).

The other component of depression is *motor*. Here again we must further dissect the syndrome into two parts: initiation of movements ("set" or preparedness) and maintenance of the activated state (locomotor activity or "drive"). During studies with L-DOPA in parkinsonian patients,[12,14] we demonstrated that initiation of movement is dependent on the striatal integration of postural, visual, and tonic reflexes and on the inhibition by nigro-striatal dopamine release of the powerful striatal inhibitory action upon the "activating" centers of the globus pallidus. [This phenomenon can be illustrated by the following analogy: suppose a car, motor running, was maintained immobile on a descending slope through the powerful pressure exerted by the foot of the driver upon the brake pedal. If the driver relaxes ("inhibits") this pressure, the "inhibition" force of the brakes becomes insufficient and the car starts to roll down the incline: this is equivalent to initiating a movement.] The resultant state of preparedness due to this double inhibition mechanism is called "set" by us. It is also evident that dopamine is the modulator of set and that a deficiency in its production results in clinical akinesia which can be corrected with L-DOPA.

On the other hand, maintenance of locomotor activity ("drive"), including its rhythmic components such as in walking, involves activation of the ascending reticular alertness system and the descending reticulo-spinal fibers acting on the segmental final common path. All the evidence points to noradrenaline as the modulator of these last components.[28] The studies of Snyder and collaborators[71] on the behavioral actions of D- and L-isomers of amphetamine indicate that this kind of locomotor hyperactivity is indeed mediated by brain norepinephrine. By contrast, the stereotyped, compulsive gnawing behavior in rats, which resembles the syndrome of Gilles de la Tourette in man, appears to be regulated by brain dopamine. L-DOPA, once it has corrected a deficient set, or akinesia, should permit increased locomotor

activity through activation of the brainstem noradrenergic systems.

In summary, if we are to understand the role of
monoamines in depression, it will be necessary to dissect
the many clinical components of the syndrome. In this
way it will become apparent that the deficiency hypothesis is probably correct if we mean by this that it can involve dopamine, noradrenaline, or serotonin, separately
or together, in one or more physiologically important
regions. At this stage in our analysis of the available
data, we think that dopamine is the modulator of the set
component of motor function. The drive component of
activity in turn is controlled and maintained by noradrenaline. *Mood,* on the other hand, could be the result of a
dynamic balance between serotoninergic and noradrenergic neuronal systems in complementary limbic and
reticular pathways which integrate the emotional and
drive components of both the external and internal
milieu.

Mania

The Schildkraut hypothesis[68] postulated that excess
of amines would be found in mania. Preliminary results
from three centers[70,72,73] confirmed these postulates but
only in some cases. Most authors, however, studied
only the urinary excretion of noradrenaline, adrenaline,
or vanilomandelic acid.

In 1970, Messiha and collaborators[55] reported that
during the manic phase there is an increase in the urinary
excretion of dopamine. Lithium carbonate, which has
been found useful in the treatment of mania, was given
to these patients and, along with favorable clinical ef-

fects, caused the dopamine excretion to return to normal. It is of interest that lithium carbonate was also found useful in a few cases of L-DOPA-treated Parkinson's disease with manic reactions,[65,67] but not in others.[74] On the other hand, Murphy and collaborators[57] reported the regular induction of hypomania by L-DOPA in "bipolar" manic-depressive patients, thus indicating that L-DOPA may reveal a previously present suscepti- bility to manic behavior.

Paul and collaborators[64] recently demonstrated that the urinary excretion of adenosine 3′,5′-cyclic mono- phosphate (cyclic AMP) was different in manic and de- pressive patients. This was confirmed by Abdulla and Hamadah.[1] Since it is most likely that the catechola- mines act through mechanisms involving cyclic AMP, these findings bear on the problem at hand, more so since it is now evident that specific dopamine-sensitive cyclic AMP receptors exist, at least in the superior cervical ganglia.[49] Dopamine may also act directly on phosphodiesterase or a specific adenyl cyclase to pro- duce its receptor action. Finally, Paul and co-work- ers[62,63] were able to increase the excretion of cyclic AMP in depressed patients given L-DOPA.

These studies all indicate that dopamine and cyclic AMP probably play a role in the pathogenesis of mania. The manic, anxious, and aggressive episodes produced by L-DOPA in humans, as well as the aggressivity, motor hyperactivity, and occasional rage seen after the same substance is given to animals, reinforce this preliminary conclusion.

Psychiatric side-effects of L-DOPA in man

During therapeutic trials with L-DOPA in Parkin- son's disease,[8,13] it has been possible to observe a constellation of acute psychiatric phenomena. At various times, or in different patients, hypomania, stereotyped behavior, paranoia, disturbed thought content, or even catatonic episodes have been documented.[66,76] In all cases this occurred with relatively high intakes of the drug and could be reversed by reducing the dosage.[31,32,43]

The first manifestations of L-DOPA overdosage are agitation, helplessness, insomnia, and irritability. Later, severe anxiety, fear, and apprehension may lead to undue euphoria or even hypomania. It is during this period that stereotypic phenomena are observed more frequently, i.e., a tendency toward bizarre, frequent, prolonged, almost mechanical aimless repetition of the same movements, postures, or behavior. From animal studies previously reported,[13,66] it appears that most stereotyped behavior is due to stimulation of dopamine receptors.

As the dose of L-DOPA is further increased, the patient may show poor judgment, anger, or even hostility sustained by definite paranoid misinterpretations. An organic confusional state manifested by hallucinations and vivid dreams will contribute toward a worsening of the paranoid features. The patient is now extremely anxious and obsessional. He may at times become violent or show antisocial behavior. One of our patients was found with a knife under his pillow which he intended to use against his roommate who, he assumed, was "going out" with his sister. Needless to say, this patient had been quite close to his sister!

In some patients, a frontal-lobe type of syndrome and lack of inhibitions will result in unacceptable behavior, particularly in the sexual sphere, with compulsive exhibitionism. In the language of the "now" generation, the patient is literally "on a trip." Compulsive behavior is quite frequent with overdosage of L-DOPA, but it is almost always coupled to stereotyped, repetitive gestures or utterances. The aimless, repetitive actions which appear to obey the compulsive dictates of the inner self, and which are seen so often in wards full of chronic schizophrenics, are occasionally observed during L-DOPA treatment.

Patients taking L-DOPA can manifest some disturbance in sensory perception. They become hyperreactive to various stimuli but the response can be inappropriate. Without demonstrating the confusion of organic mental states, some patients become disoriented as to time and place. They act as if they were actually living a few years back, or under other conditions. One of our patients, after inadvertently taking a double dose of DOPA at lunch time, and subsequently being involved in an argument with his boss, drove home without difficulty in a red Cadillac which did not belong to him and which he had found in the company garage. It turns out, however, that a few years previously he had owned an identical car. When he arrived home, he related to his wife as current some events which had actually happened at the time he owned that car. This type of time dissociation is quite rare, but it has great theoretical importance in view of the fact that it had never occurred in this patient, and has not reappeared since that one episode.

Finally, when L-DOPA is given at a very high dosage, and maintained at such levels without surveillance for long periods of time, a definite catatonic syndrome may be seen. Two patients treated elsewhere with 10 and 12 g daily of L-DOPA were referred to us for evaluation. Neither had seen his physician in the preceding

6 months, but both had continued on the same dosage. When examined, they presented all the features of classical catatonia, except for the muscle tone and the deep tendon reflexes, which were reduced. This state disappeared within 1 month upon reduction of the dose to 4 g daily, with return of the muscle tone and reflexes to normal.

Thus it is possible with L-DOPA to mimic many diverse presentations of the toxic mental syndrome as recently reviewed by Goodwin.[46] How DOPA, dopamine, or some other metabolite does this is still unclear, but these observations again point to a possible role of dopamine in some mental disorders.[76]

Further support for this hypothesis can be derived from the fact that the drugs found to be the most effective in many mental disorders, i.e., the phenothiazines and butyrophenones,[34] are both known to block dopamine receptors and to increase the turnover of dopamine to homovanillic acid (HVA).[2,77]

More long-term experience with L-DOPA in Parkinson's disease has permitted the delineation of certain heretofore unusual manifestations in the mental sphere.[11] These include subtle changes in cortical function, evidenced by a gradual decrease in the attention span (particularly directed attention) and, occasionally, loss of memory for recent events. These symptoms are also signs of advancing age and cerebral arteriosclerosis, but they seem to appear anew with surprising frequency in the short span of 2 years. In some patients, modifications in social behavior were also observed which are best described as frontal-lobe-like "insouciance." Although general intellectual abilities appeared intact, relatives and friends noted changes in behavior, particularly in the sexual sphere. This chronic behavior change was distinct from the acute psychotic manifestations of overdosage previously described. As will be seen later, the many known effects of L-DOPA on protein synthesis, S-adenosyl-methionine, and many other neurotransmitter systems may be involved in these behavior changes; however, it is still possible that the only factor to be considered should be the unmasking of the natural progression of the illness.

PATHOGENESIS OF MENTAL DISORDERS AS RELATED TO DOPAMINE

From the above clinical evidence, it is concluded that a deficiency in dopamine may be involved in the set motor component of the depressive syndrome and may also be related, through its complementary effects on the metabolism of serotonin and noradrenaline, to the mechanism of mood and drive. Similarly, there is evidence that the hyperactivity and aggressiveness of manic episodes are the result of overstimulation of dopamine receptors.

How dopamine exerts its action upon mental functions is still unknown, but, if we accept that it has some role to play, a number of possibilities can be considered.

(1) Dopamine could directly enhance inhibitory mechanisms in various circuits including the striatum.

(2) High dopamine contents could unsettle the delicate balance with other postulated neurotransmitters (noradrenaline, serotonin, acetylcholine, gamma-aminobutyric acid).[22] This could involve one of four

mechanisms, all of which have been demonstrated to be possible.

    (a) competition for transport, uptake, or storage mechanisms;[15,78]

    (b) "false transmitter" effect (displacement);[58]

    (c) release or interference with other transmitters or with important enzymes or co-enzymes;[39,45]

    (d) change in turnover rates of other amines.[59]

(3) Dopamine could form abnormal metabolites. This may involve abnormal methylation,[5,6,9] abnormal transamination, or formation in abnormal quantity of compounds usually in low concentration which in turn could unsettle other amines.[20,41,48,53] The latest compound to receive attention as a possible cause of mental symptoms is 6-hydroxy-dopamine, but there is no evidence yet that it can be found *in vivo* in normal or diseased brains.

(4) Dopamine could act indirectly: increased requirements for methyl groups,[75] as well as deficiencies in S-adenosyl-methionine[75] and in catechol-O-methyl-transferase (COMT) have indeed been noted after L-DOPA treatment.[45]

(5) Finally, dopamine could exert its effects by directly influencing the cyclic AMP system and its many components.[49,62,64]

Despite the above-noted uncertainty on the exact mechanism of its action, we feel the available evidence is sufficiently strong to warrant further detailed studies on the role of dopamine in the pathogenesis of many mental disorders.

ROLE OF THE STRIATUM IN MENTAL FUNCTION

Implicating dopamine in normal and abnormal mental functions automatically draws attention to two areas of the brain where this amine is found in the highest concentrations — the striatum (caudate nucleus and putamen) and the median eminence of the hypothalamus. Following the same reasoning, disturbances in serotonin and noradrenaline would mainly implicate the limbic system, the hypothalamus, and the brainstem. The median eminence of the hypothalamus is involved in the control of peptidic releasing and inhibitory factors which in turn regulate pituitary hormone release; thus it is concerned with neuroendocrine regulation, one aspect of the total autonomic response of the organism. It is well known that the brainstem is intimately related to many other autonomic responses, e.g., breathing, heart rate, blood pressure.

In two recent papers[12,14] we have reviewed the role of the striatum in the feedback control of the autonomic and endocrine components of nervous system. We have shown that somehow, through neural and humoral long and short feedback loops, the striatum is informed of the state of activity, and balance, of the sympathetic and parasympathetic autonomic nervous systems at the periphery, within the hypothalamus and within the brainstem. When these two systems are in functional balance, the striatum is essentially passive and quiescent. However, when there is an imbalance between the tropotrophic and the ergotrophic system in either of these areas, the striatum reacts by activating the turnover of dopamine, which in turn modifies the metabolism of other systems (serotonin, noradrenaline). It has been shown[12,14] that striatal dopamine turnover is the pivoting mechanism for feedback integration and correction of homeostatic imbalances.

The striatum has been implicated in mental function for many years, particularly by Mettler and his group.[52,56] The evidence reviewed in this chapter adds further weight to this intriguing possibility. If such is the case, dopamine is probably the main substance involved. Recent studies by Bliss and Ailion[18] indicate that the metabolism of dopamine is indeed accelerated by a variety of behaviors. These authors have shown that emotionally disturbing experiences, either when they are accompanied by augmented activity or when they are unassociated with it, will increase the metabolism of dopamine. In turn, an increase in activity in the absence of stress will again accelerate the metabolism of dopamine.

To date we have put emphasis mainly on the motor and external behavioral aspects of mental function. In a recent study, Botez and I[19] have reviewed the role of subcortical structures in the mechanism of speech, one of the highest intellectual functions of man. It was shown that speech, as the output side of information processing and the vehicle of language, requires constant modulation and control from subcortical mechanisms. After stereotaxic operations creating lesions in the so-called striatal loop output (in globus pallidus or VL nucleus of thalamus), the fluency of speech is often involved, but the conceptual system for language remains intact.

Studies on cognitive changes before and after L-DOPA, such as those by Beardsley and Puletti[16] and others,[50] are still inconclusive. It is not yet possible to establish definitive patterns in I.Q. changes, and it is probable that it will be necessary to use much finer psychometric tests to form an opinion. However, we are certain that it will eventually be shown that many cortical cognitive parameters are directly under the modulating influence of cortico-subcortical loops[19] and that in these reverberating circuits the striatum, with its dominant dopamine metabolism, will play an important controlling role.

SUMMARY

The present study reviews the recent evidence which delineates a possible role for dopamine in the pathogenesis of some mental disorders. A deficiency in dopamine could be involved in the set (or preparedness) component of the motor aspects of depression, whereas overstimulation of specific dopamine receptors probably is concerned with hypomania and stereotyped behavior. Overdosage with L-DOPA can result in acute or chronic syndromes ranging from vivid dreams to complete catatonia. It is proposed that the striatum plays an important modulating role on many components of mental activity and that this function is accomplished mainly through modifications in the striatal turnover of dopamine.

ACKNOWLEDGMENTS

The studies in the author's laboratory referred to in this paper were supported over the years by the Medical Research Council of Canada, the Department of National Health and Welfare of Canada, the Huntington's Chorea Foundation, the Committee to Combat

Huntington's Disease, the W. Garfield Weston Foundation, and an award from the Canadian Mental Health Association.

REFERENCES

1. Abdulla, Y. H., and Hamadah, K. (1970): 3′5′-Cyclic adenosine monophosphate in depression and mania. *Lancet,* 1:378–381.

2. Andén, N. E., Roos, B. E., and Werdinius, B. (1964): Effects of chlorpromazine, haloperidol and reserpine on the levels of phenolic acids in rabbit corpus striatum. *Life Sciences,* 3:149–158.

3. Ashcroft, G. W., Crawford, T. B. B., Eccleston, D., Sharman, D. F., MacDougall, E. J., Stanton, J. B., and Binns, J. K. (1966): 5-Hydroxyindole compounds in the cerebrospinal fluid of patients with psychiatric or neurological disease. *Lancet,* 2:1049.

4. Barbeau, A., Murphy, G. F., and Sourkes, T. L. (1961): Excretion of dopamine in diseases of basal ganglia. *Science,* 133:1706–1707.

5. Barbeau, A., Tetreault, L., Oliva, L., Morazain, L., and Cardin, L. (1966): Pharmacology of akinesia: Investigations on 3,4-dimethoxyphenylethylamine. *Nature,* 209:719–721.

6. Barbeau, A. (1967): The 'pink spot,' 3,4-dimethoxyphenylethylamine and dopamine. Relationship to Parkinson's disease and to schizophrenia. *Rev. Can. Biol.,* 26:55–79.

7. Barbeau, A. (1968): Effect of phenothiazines on dopamine metabolism and biochemistry of Parkinson's disease. *Agressologie,* 9:195–200.

8. Barbeau, A. (1969): L-DOPA therapy in Parkinson's disease: A critical review of nine years' experience. *Can. Med. Ass. J.,* 101:791–800.

9. Barbeau, A. (1970): L-DOPA and abnormal methylation. In: *L-DOPA and Parkinsonism,* edited by A. Barbeau and F. H. McDowell. F. A. Davis, Philadelphia, pp. 360–362.

10. Barbeau, A. (1970): Dopamine and disease. *Can. Med. Ass. J.,* 103:824–832.

11. Barbeau, A. (1971): Long-term side-effects of levodopa. *Lancet,* 1:395.

12. Barbeau, A. (1971): Functions of the striatum; a new proposal based on experience with L-DOPA in extrapyramidal disorders. In: *Monoamines, Noyaux Gris Centraux et Syndrome de Parkinson,* edited by J. de Ajuriaguerra and G. Gauthier, Masson & Cie, Paris, pp. 451–454.

13. Barbeau, A., Mars, H., and Gillo-Joffroy, L. (1971): Adverse clinical side-effects of levodopa therapy. In: *Recent Advances in Parkinson's Disease,* edited by F. H. McDowell and C. H. Markham. F. A. Davis, Philadelphia, pp. 203–237.

14. Barbeau, A. (1972): Role of dopamine in the nervous system. In: *Monographs in Human Genetics,* Vol. 6, edited by J. François. S. Karger, Basel, pp. 114–136.

15. Bartholini, G., and Pletscher, A. (1968): Cerebral accumulation and metabolism of C^{14}-DOPA after selective inhibition of peripheral decarboxylase. *J. Pharmacol. Exp. Ther.,* 161:14–20.

16. Beardsley, J. V., and Puletti, F. (1971): Personality (MMPI) and cognitive (WAIS) changes after levodopa treatment. *Arch. Neurol.,* 25:145–150.

17. Bertler, A., and Rosengren, E. (1959): Occurence and distribution of dopamine in brain and other tissues. *Experientia,* 15:10–11.

18. Bliss, E. L., and Ailion, J. (1971): Relationship of stress and activity to brain dopamine and homovanillic acid. *Life Sciences,* 10:1161–1169.

19. Botez, M. I., and Barbeau, A. (1972): Role of subcortical structures, and particularly of the thalamus, in the mechanisms of speech and language — A review. *Int. J. Neurol. (in press).*

20. Boulton, A. A., and Quan, L. (1969): The presence and distribution of p-tyramine in rat brain. In: *Proc. 2nd Int. Meeting Int. Soc. Neurochemistry,* Milan, pp. 101–102.

21. Brodie, B. B., and Reid, W. D. (1968): Serotonin in brain: Functional considerations. *Adv. Pharmacol.,* 6B:97.

22. Bryson, G. (1971): Biogenic amines in normal and abnormal behavioral states. *Clin. Chem.,* 17:5–26.

23. Bunney, W. E., Janowsky, D. S., Goodwin, F. K., Davis, J. M., Brodie, H. K. H., Murphy, D. L., and Chase, T. N. (1969): Effect of L-DOPA on depression. *Lancet,* 1:885–886.

24. Bunney, W. E. (1970): Present status of psychological reactions to L-DOPA. *Amer. J. Psychiat.,* 127:361–362.

25. Bunney, W. E., Murphy, D. L., Brodie, H. K. H., and Goodwin, F. K. (1970): L-DOPA in depressed patients. *Lancet,* 1:352.

26. Butcher, L. L., and Engel, J. (1969): Behavioral and biochemical effects of L-DOPA after peripheral decarboxylase inhibition. *Brain Res.,* 15:233–242.

27. Carlsson, A. (1959): The occurrence, distribution and physiological role of catecholamines in the nervous system. *Pharmacol. Rev.,* 11:490–493.

28. Carlsson, A., Falck, B., Fuxe, K., and Hillarp, N. (1964): Cellular localization of monoamines in the spinal cord. *Acta Physiol. Scand.,* 60:112–119.

29. Chalmers, J. P., Baldessarini, R. J., and Wurtman, R. J. (1971): Effects of L-DOPA on brain norepinephrine metabolism. *Proc. Nat. Acad. Sci.,* 68:662–666.

30. Cherington, M. (1970): Parkinsonism, L-DOPA and mental depression. *J. Amer. Geriat. Soc.,* 18:513–516.

31. Clark, W. G. (1970): Some aspects of the pharmacology of the psychic and behavioral effects of L-3,4-dihydroxyphenylalanine (L-DOPA). In: *L-DOPA and Parkinsonism,* edited by A. Barbeau and F. H. McDowell. F. A. Davis, Philadelphia, pp. 349–359.

32. Cole, J. O. (1970): Psychiatric aspects of L-DOPA treatment. In: *L-DOPA and Parkinsonism,* edited by A. Barbeau and F. H. McDowell. F. A. Davis, Philadelphia, pp. 363–364.

33. Coppen, A., Shaw, D. M., and Farrell, J. P. (1963): Potentiation of the antidepressive effect of a monoamine oxidase inhibitor by tryptophane. *Lancet,* 1:79.

34. Crane, G. E. (1967): A review of clinical literature on haloperidol. *J. Neuropsychiat.,* 3 (suppl. 1):110–127.

35. DeGroot, J. A., and Barbeau, A. (1966): The problem of measurement of akinesia. *J. Neurosurg.,* 24:331–334.

36. Degwitz, R., Frowein, R., Kulenkampf, C., and Mohs, V.

(1960): Uber die Wirkungen des L-DOPA beim Menschen und deren Beeinflussung durch Reserpin, Chlorpromazin, Iproniazid und Vitamin B$_6$. *Klin. Wschr.*, 38:120–123.

37. Dencker, S. J., Malm, V., Roos, B. E., and Werdinius, B. (1966): Acid monoamine metabolites of cerebrospinal fluid in mental depression and mania. *J. Neurochem.*, 13:1545–1548.

38. Dery, J. P., DeGroot, J. A., Laurin, C., and Barbeau, A. (1962): Nouvelle méthode d'évaluation objective de la rigidité et du tremblement dans la maladie de Parkinson. *Union Med. Can.*, 91:842–847.

39. Dunner, D. L., Cohn, C. K., Gershon, E. S., and Goodwin, F. K. (1971): Differential catechol/O-methyltransferase activity in unipolar and bipolar affective illness. *Arch. Gen. Psychiat.*, 25:348–353.

40. Ehringer, H., and Hornykiewicz, O. (1960): Verteilung von Noradrenalin und Dopamin (3-hydroxytyramine) im Gehirn des Menschen und ihr Verhalten bei Erkrankungen des extrapyramidalen Systems. *Klin. Wschr.*, 38:1236–1239.

41. Ernst, A. M. (1969): The role of biogenic amines in the extrapyramidal system. *Acta Physiol. Pharmacol. Neerl.*, 15:141–154.

42. Everett, G. M., and Toman, J. E. P. (1959): Mode of action of rauwolfia alkaloids and motor activity. In: *Biological Psychiatry*, edited by J. H. Masserman. Grune and Stratton, New York, pp. 75–81.

43. Everett, G. M. (1970): Evidence for dopamine as a central neuromodulator: Neurological and behavioral implications.

In: L-*DOPA and Parkinsonism,* edited by A. Barbeau and F. H. McDowell. F. A. Davis, Philadelphia, pp. 364–368.

44. Everett, G. M., and Borcherding, J. W. (1970): L-DOPA: Effect on concentrations of dopamine, norepinephrine and serotonin in brains of mice. *Science,* 168:849–850.

45. Frère, J. M., and Barbeau, A. (1971): Blood catechol-O-methyltransferase activity in Parkinson's disease. *Lancet,* 2:269–270.

46. Goodwin, F. K. (1971): Psychiatric side-effects of levodopa in man. *J.A.M.A.,* 218:1915–1920.

47. Hornykiewicz, O. (1966): Dopamine (3-hydroxytyramine) and brain function. *Pharmacol. Rev.,* 18:925–964.

48. Jonas, W., and Scheel-Kruger, J. (1969): Amphetamine-induced stereotyped behavior correlated with the accumulation of O-methylated dopamine. *Arch. Int. Pharmacodyn.,* 177: 379–389.

49. Kebabian, J. W., and Greengard, P. (1971): Dopamine-sensitive adenyl-cyclase: Possible role in synaptic transmission. *Science,* 174:1346–1349.

50. Klaiber, R., Siegfried, J., Ziegler, W. H., and Perret, E. (1971): Psychomotor effects of L-DOPA combined with a decarboxylase inhibitor on parkinsonian patients. *Europ. J. Clin. Pharmacol.,* 3:172–175.

51. Klerman, G. L., Schildkraut, J. J., Hasenbush, L. L., Greenblatt, M., and Friend, D. G. (1963): Clinical experience with dihydroxyphenylalanine (DOPA) in depression. *J. Psychiat. Res.,* 1:289–297.

52. Kline, N. S., and Mettler, F. A. (1961): The extrapyramidal system and schizophrenia. In: *Extrapyramidal System and Neuroleptics,* edited by J. M. Bordeleau. Presses Université de Montréal, Montréal, pp. 487, 491.

53. Kuehl, F. A., Vandenheuvel, W. J. A., and Ormond, R. E. (1968): Urinary metabolites in Parkinson's disease. *Nature,* 217:136–138.

54. Lemieux, G., Davignon, A., and Genest, J. (1956): Depressive states during rauwolfia therapy for arterial hypertension. *Can. Med. Ass. J.,* 74:522–526.

55. Messiha, F. S., Agallianos, D., and Clower, C. (1970): Dopamine excretion in affective states and following Li_2CO_3 therapy. *Nature,* 225:868.

56. Mettler, F. A., and Crandell, A. (1959): Relation between parkinsonism and psychiatric disorder. *J. Nerv. Ment. Dis.,* 129:551–563.

57. Murphy, D. L., Brodie, H. K. H., Goodwin, F. K., and Bunney, W. E. (1971): Regular induction of hypomania by L-DOPA in "bipolar" manic-depressive patients. *Nature,* 229:135–136.

58. Ng, K. Y., Chase, T. N., Colburn, R. W., and Kopin, I. J. (1970): L-DOPA-induced release of cerebral monoamines. *Science,* 170:76–77.

59. Orzeck, A., and Barbeau, A. (1970): Interrelationships between dopamine, serotonin and acetylcholine. In: *L-DOPA and Parkinsonism,* edited by A. Barbeau and F. H. McDowell. F. A. Davis, Philadelphia, pp. 88–94.

60. Papeschi, R., and McClure, D. J. (1971): Homovanillic and 5-hydroxyindoleacetic acid in cerebrospinal fluid of depressed patients. *Arch. Gen. Psychiat.*, 25:354–358.

61. Pare, C. M. B., and Sandler, M. (1959): A clinical and biochemical study of a trial of iproniazid in the treatment of depression. *J. Neurol. Neurosurg. Psychiat.*, 22:247–251.

62. Paul, M. I., Cramer, H., and Goodwin, F. K. (1970): Urinary cyclic AMP in affective illness. *Lancet*, 1:996.

63. Paul, M. I., Cramer, H., and Goodwin, F. K. (1970): Urinary cyclic AMP excretion in depression and mania. *Arch. Gen. Psychiat.*, 24:327–333.

64. Paul, M. I., Ditzion, B. R., and Janowsky, D. S. (1970): Affective illness and cyclic AMP excretion. *Lancet*, 1:88.

65. Pearlman, C. A. (1971): Manic behavior and levodopa. *New Engl. J. Med.*, 285:1326.

66. Randrup, A., and Munkrad, I. (1967): Stereotyped activities produced by amphetamine in several animal species and man. *Psychopharmacologia*, 11:300–310.

67. Ryback, R. S., and Schwab, R. S. (1971): Manic response to levodopa therapy. *New Engl. J. Med.*, 285:788–789.

68. Schildkraut, J. J. (1965): The catecholamine hypothesis of affective disorders: A review of supporting evidence. *Amer. J. Psychiat.*, 122:509–522.

69. Shaw, D. M., Camps, F., and Eccleston, E. G. (1967): 5-Hydroxytryptamine in the hindbrain of depressive suicides. *Brit. J. Psychiat.*, 113:1407.

70. Shinfuku, N., Omura, M., and Kayano, M. (1961): Cate-

cholamines in manic depressive illness. *Yonango Acta Med.,* 5:109.

71. Snyder, S. H., Taylor, K. M., Coyle, J. T., and Meyerhoff, J. L. (1970): The role of brain dopamine in behavioral regulation and the actions of psychotropic drugs. *Amer. J. Psychiat.,* 127:199–207.

72. Stroem-Olsen, R., and Weil-Malherbe, H. (1958): Catecholamines in mania. *J. Ment. Sci.,* 104:696.

73. Takahashi, R., Nagao, Y., Tsuchiya, K., Takamizawa, M., Kobayashi, T., Toru, M., Kobayashi, K., and Kariya, T. (1968): Catecholamine metabolism of manic depressive illness. *J. Psychiat. Res.,* 6:185.

74. VanWoert, M. H., Ambani, L. M., and Weintraub, M. I. (1971): Manic behavior and levodopa. *New Engl. J. Med.,* 285:1326.

75. Wurtman, R. J., Rose, C. M., Matthysse, S., Stephenson, J., and Baldessarini, R. (1970): L-Dihydroxyphenylalanine: Effect on S-adenosylmethionine in brain. *Science,* 169:395–397.

76. Yaryura-Tobias, J. A., Diamond, B., and Merlis, S. (1970): The action of L-DOPA on schizophrenic patients (a preliminary report). *Current Ther. Res.,* 12:528–531.

77. Yeh, B. K., McNay, J. L., and Goldberg, L. I. (1969): Attenuation of dopamine renal and mesenteric vasodilation by haloperidol: Evidence for a specific dopamine receptor. *J. Pharmacol. Exp. Ther.,* 168:303–309.

78. Yuwiler, A., Geller, E., and Eiduson, S. (1959): Studies on 5-hydroxytryptophan decarboxylase. I. In vivo inhibition and substrate interaction. *Arch. Biochem.,* 80:162–173.

Brain Dopamine and Behavior

Solomon H. Snyder, Alan S. Horn, Kenneth M. Taylor, and Joseph T. Coyle

Of the two catecholamines (Fig. 1), norepinephrine has, until very recently, received the lion's share of attention. Many drugs which altered tissue levels of dopamine as well as norepinephrine, not to mention serotonin, were always presumed, without any second thoughts, to exert their psychotropic actions via the favored norepinephrine. In most discussions of mood, reserpine, monoamine oxidase inhibitors, or tricyclic antidepressants, norepinephrine has been the darling of the psychopharmacologists. Only with the advent of the almost miraculous therapeutic success of L-dihydroxy-phenylalanine (L-DOPA) in Parkinson's disease and the demonstration of the depletion of dopamine in the corpus striatum of patients suffering from this disease has dopamine come in for its proper share of attention.

A major task which must be completed before deciding whether to attribute a given behavioral or drug effect to one or the other of the catecholamines is to find agents which will discriminate between dopamine and norepinephrine neurons in the brain. In this chapter we describe recent studies in this laboratory which show differences between the biochemical properties and interactions with drugs of norepinephrine and dopamine nerve terminals. Studies contrasting the biochemical and behavioral effects of the two isomers of amphetamine have been especially useful in differentiating between behaviors attributable to dopamine or to norepinephrine. Examination of structure: activity relationships of a number of tricyclic agents in inhibiting catecholamine uptake by norepinephrine or dopamine nerve terminals suggests new drugs which might be specific in affecting the functioning of one or the other of these neuronal classes. Finally, a comparison of the relative potencies of *d*- and *l*-isomers of tranylcypromine (Parnate®) in inhibiting monoamine oxidase (MAO) activity and in blocking catecholamine uptake suggests a means of testing as to which of these processes the antidepressant efficacy of this drug is related.

DIFFERENCES IN CATECHOLAMINE UPTAKE BY NOREPINEPHRINE AND DOPAMINE NEURONS

A major tool in studying the biochemical characteristics of catecholamine neurons in our laboratory has been examination of amine uptake by synaptosomes (pinched-off nerve endings). It is generally accepted that this uptake process serves to inactivate synaptically released catecholamines. We have found it possible to examine kinetics of the uptake process efficiently *in vitro* using crude preparations of synaptosomes.[1,12-14] One can readily compare catecholamine uptake by dopamine and norepinephrine neurons using the corpus striatum (in which 95% of the catecholamine content is dopamine) as an example of dopaminergic neurons while almost any other brain region contains primarily norepinephrine neurons. In this way we were able to compare the stereospecificity of catecholamine uptake by norepinephrine and dopamine neurons and observed interesting differences which may have significant clinical implications.

Because the beta-hydroxyl group of norepinephrine creates an asymmetric center, this molecule has two stereoisomers of which *l*-norepinephrine is the naturally occurring form (Fig. 1). Dopamine, lacking a substituent at the beta position, occurs in only one stereoisomeric form. In several norepinephrine brain regions of the rat, monkey, and guinea pig, the naturally occurring *l*-norepinephrine showed four times greater affinity than the *d*-isomer.[1] On the other hand, in the corpus striatum, a dopaminergic area, there was no difference in the affinities of *d*- or *l*-norepinephrine for the catecholamine uptake system. It seemed as if the membranes of the

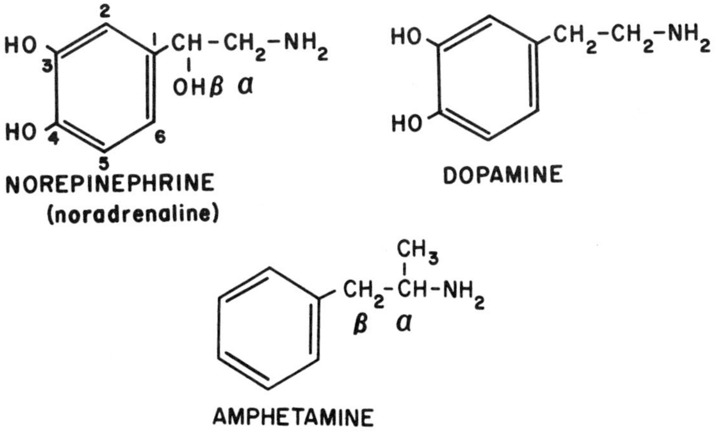

FIG. 1. Structures of norepinephrine, dopamine, and amphetamine.

dopamine neurons of the striatum had been created with no preference for *d-* or *l*-norepinephrine, i.e., at the beta carbon, "because" they had no need to make such a distinction in recapturing their "symmetric" transmitter, dopamine, after its synaptic release.

To examine the stereospecificity of dopamine and norepinephrine neuron uptake processes at the alpha carbon, the effects of *d-* and *l*-amphetamine on catecholamine uptake were compared. Amphetamine has a methyl group at the alpha carbon so that there are two isomeric forms, of which *d*-amphetamine has the greater central stimulant properties. *d*-Amphetamine inhibits catecholamine uptake, and it has been postulated that resultant potentiation of synaptically released catecholamine could account for its central stimulant properties. In the cerebral cortex and hypothalamus, predominantly norepinephrine regions, *d*-amphetamine was ten times as potent an inhibitor of catecholamine uptake as *l*-amphetamine.[1,15] However, in the corpus striatum, the *d-* and *l*-amphetamines were equally active inhibitors of catecholamine uptake, and both were more potent than *d*-amphetamine in norepinephrine areas. Thus, stereospecificity at both alpha and beta carbons exists in norepinephrine neurons and is absent in the dopamine neurons. The potential clinical relevance of these findings will become evident after considering the effects of known anti-parkinsonian drugs on catecholamine uptake.

First, however, to make sure that these *in vitro* findings could be extended to intact animals, the effects of *d-* and *l*-amphetamine administered to rats *in vivo* were studied on the uptake of intraventricularly injected ^{3}H-catecholamines and on their endogenous levels.[17]

TABLE 1. *Inhibition of ³H-norepinephrine uptake into brain regions by d- and l-amphetamine*

Brain region	Treatment	Endogenous norepinephrine (µg/g)	Endogenous dopamine (µg/g)	³H-Norepinephrine c/min/g $\times 10^4$
striatum	saline	0.09 ± 0.01	4.44 ± 0.25	159 ± 4
	d-amphetamine	0.08 ± 0.01	4.36 ± 0.30	79 ± 6*
	l-amphetamine	0.09 ± 0.01	4.69 ± 0.32	86 ± 4*
thalamus-hypothalamus-midbrain	saline	0.61 ± 0.03		221 ± 9
	d-amphetamine	0.44 ± 0.04*		160 ± 8*
	l-amphetamine	0.59 ± 0.03		211 ± 12
cerebellum	saline	0.35 ± 0.01		383 ± 17
	d-amphetamine	0.20 ± 0.01*		198 ± 23*
	l-amphetamine	0.33 ± 0.01		348 ± 20
brain stem	saline	0.42 ± 0.04		160 ± 27
	d-amphetamine	0.33 ± 0.02**		99 ± 23**
	l-amphetamine	0.44 ± 0.02		160 ± 27

Rats were pretreated with d- or l-amphetamine (10 mg/kg s.c.) 1 hr before the intraventricular injection of 20 µC (20 µl) of ³H-norepinephrine. All rats were decapitated 5 min after ³H-norepinephrine administration, their brains removed, dissected, and endogenous and ³H-norepinephrine determined. Control animals received 0.9% NaCl solution in place of amphetamine. Each value is the mean ± S.E.M. of eight determinations. Significance of difference between mean treated and control.

* < 0.001.

** < 0.05.

In the cerebellum, the hypothalamus, thalamus, midbrain, and the brain-stem, *d*-amphetamine caused a marked reduction in the accumulation of the ^{3}H-norepinephrine whereas *l*-amphetamine had no effect (Table 1). Because rats were killed soon (5 min) after injection of ^{3}H-norepinephrine, the effect of amphetamine on amine accumulation is probably related to inhibition of neuronal membrane uptake rather than to effects on granular retention or amine release. *d*-Amphetamine but not *l*-amphetamine lowered endogenous norepinephrine concentration in these areas. In the corpus striatum, however, both *d*- and *l*-amphetamine caused marked reductions in accumulation of ^{3}H-norepinephrine without affecting endogenous dopamine or norepinephrine concentrations (Table 1). These findings confirm *in vivo* our earlier findings *in vitro* that in nonstriatal synaptosomes *d*-amphetamine is a much more potent inhibitor of catecholamine accumulation than is *l*-amphetamine. We also confirm *in vivo* that *d*- and *l*-amphetamine inhibit to the same degree the accumulation of catecholamines into striatal synaptosomes.

ANTI-PARKINSONIAN DRUG ACTION: CATECHOLAMINE UPTAKE INHIBITION AS A POSSIBLE MECHANISM

Many anti-parkinsonian drugs are anticholinergic agents, and it has often been presumed that acetylcholine receptor blockade mediated their clinical efficacy. However, some anti-parkinsonian drugs, such as the antihistamine diphenhydramine (Benadryl®) are fairly weak anticholinergic agents. We observed that a variety of anti-parkinsonian agents, be they anticholinergics, antihistamines, indole derivatives, or phenothiazines, were potent inhibitors of striatal catecholamine uptake in synaptosomal preparations.[2] Some of these drugs, such as benztropine (Cogentin®) and trihexyphenidyl (Artane®), were 10 to 20 times more potent inhibitors of catecholamine uptake in the striatum than in the hypothalamus. Their preferential action on dopamine neurons contrasts strikingly with the selective effect on norepinephrine neurons of some antidepressants. Desmethylimipramine, for instance, was about 1,000 times more active in inhibiting catecholamine uptake in norepinephrine areas than in the dopaminergic corpus straitum. These observations suggest that these anti-parkinsonian drugs may owe their therapeutic efficacy, at least in part, to inhibition of striatal dopamine uptake.[2] By inhibiting re-uptake of dopamine, the anti-parkinsonian drugs would potentiate the effects of dopamine released at striatal synapses and tend to counteract the dopamine deficiency in the brains of patients with Parkinson's disease.

In light of this hypothesis for the mechanism of action of anti-parkinsonian drugs, the absence of stereospecificity of amphetamine in its actions on dopamine neurons takes on therapeutic implication. *d*-Amphetamine has been used in the therapy of Parkinson's disease, but its central stimulant effects have restricted the dosage to low levels. *l*-Amphetamine is a much weaker central stimulant. This model suggests that the therapeutic actions of *d*-amphetamine in this disease are related to inhibition of catecholamine uptake in the striatum. Since *d*- and *l*-amphetamines are equally potent inhibitors of catecholamine uptake in the striatum, *l*-amphetamine should have equal anti-parkinsonian activity. However, it can be administered in higher doses with fewer central stimulant side effects than *d*-amphetamine and, accordingly, should be a more powerful therapeutic agent. As a test of this hypothesis, the ability of predicted anti-parkinsonian agents to prevent the tremor produced by oxotremorine was studied.[2] The effects in animals of oxotremorine resemble Parkinson's disease, and the clinical efficacy of anti-parkinsonian drugs is closely paralleled by their ability to prevent the oxotremorine syndrome. In support of this prediction, *d*- and *l*-amphetamines were found to be equally active in preventing the tremor and rigidity produced in mice by oxotremorine.[2]

STRUCTURE: ACTIVITY RELATIONS OF INHIBITORS OF CATECHOLAMINE UPTAKE

It is unlikely that inhibition of catecholamine uptake in the corpus striatum itself is sufficient to account for the clinical efficacy of anti-parkinsonian drugs. When we began screening a larger number of drugs, it became apparent that some compounds which are fairly good anti-parkinsonian drugs, such as atropine and scopolamine, are relatively weak catecholamine uptake inhibitors, although they do show this activity.

In such screenings we were able to determine the chemical characteristics which seem most important for inhibition of catecholamine uptake, and, more interestingly, those characteristics which selectively increase affinity of drugs for norepinephrine or dopamine neurons, respectively.[8]

One question readily answered was why the anti-parkinsonian drugs should have any effect on catecholamine uptake processes; or, more simply, is there any relationship between their ability to inhibit catecholamine uptake and the well-known catecholamine uptake inhibition mediated by the tricyclic antidepressants? The answer is yes. Most anti-parkinsonian drugs contain two aromatic rings and their relationship to each other, as shown in Fig. 2 for benztropine, tends to mimic the three rings of the tricyclic agents.

BENZTROPINE

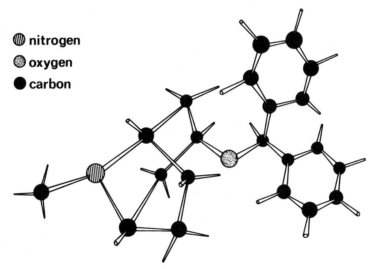

FIG. 2. A molecular model of benztropine (Cogentin®) in what is proposed to be its preferred conformation.

Benztropine was the most potent inhibitor of catecholamine uptake in the corpus striatum of drugs examined, and it was more than 20 times as active in the striatum as in the hypothalamus (Fig. 3).[8] Comparing a number of analogs led us to conclude that the tropine

TROPINES

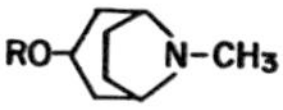

NAME	R	RELATIVE POTENCY STRIATUM (S)	HYPOTHALAMUS (H)	S/H
BENZTROPINE	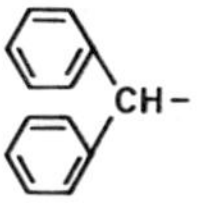	8,333	370	22.5
BS 6825	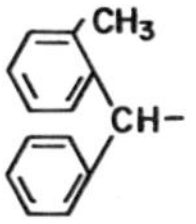	2,000	100	20.0
DEPTROPINE	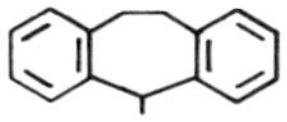	1,333	143	9.3
BS 7039	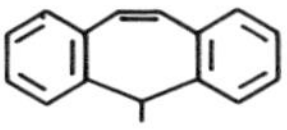	1,000	33	30.3
BS 7723	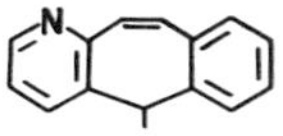	167	10	16.7
BS 7042	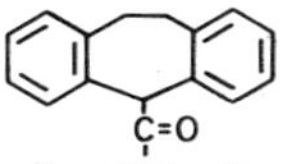	100	100	1.0
BS 7715	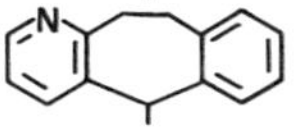	50	15	3.3
ATROPINE	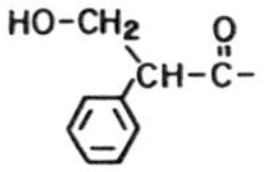	20	12	1.6
SCOPOLAMINE	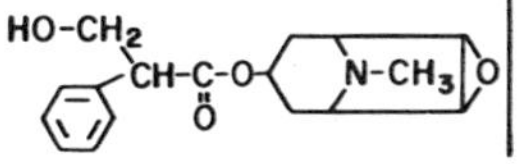	5	3	1.6

FIG. 3. Structure: activity relationships of tropine analogs in inhibiting catecholamine uptake by dopamine synaptosomes prepared from the corpus striatum, and those from the hypothalamus, presumably noradrenergic. Potency values are expressed as the reciprocal of the dose required to inhibit catecholamine uptake 50%. A potency of 1 corresponds to an ID_{50} value of 10^{-3}M. S/H is the ratio of potencies in striatum and hypothalamus.

side chain is an important determinant of this selective effect on the dopamine neurons of the corpus striatum. For instance, deptropine and B.S. 7039 resemble nortriptyline and protriptyline, respectively, but have considerably greater selective effects on catecholamine uptake in the corpus striatum. This seems to be related solely to the fact that they have tropine side chains.

Another interesting observation was that, all other things being equal, drugs with only two aromatic rings tend to be more active than comparable chemicals in which the two rings are bridged together to form a tricyclic compound. Examples of this phenomenon are the greater activity of benztropine than the tricyclic compounds, deptropine, and B.S. 7039 (Fig. 3).

Our screening experiments also revealed interesting features about the actions of antidepressant agents.[8] It has long been thought that tertiary amines such as imipramine were "activated" by demethylation to form secondary amines such as desipramine. The evidence for this was that in some animal tests desipramine seems to be a more potent antidepressant than imipramine, and it also is a more active inhibitor of catecholamine uptake by norepinephrine neurons (Fig. 4). It is striking how selective desipramine is for norepinephrine neurons, being about 1,000 times as active on them as on dopamine neurons. We were quite surprised to find that this axiom failed when we examined the well-known antidepressant amitriptyline (Elavil®) and its secondary amine nortriptyline (Aventyl®); in this case, the tertiary amine amitriptyline was more than 20 times as potent on hypothalamic norepinephrine neurons as its demethylated derivative. Like desipramine, amitriptyline showed a pronounced selectivity for norepinephrine neurons (Fig. 4).

TRICYCLICS

RELATIVE POTENCY

NAME	A	B	R	STRIATUM (S)	HYPOTHALAMUS (H)	S/H
60-389 a	—	N	-(CH$_2$)$_3$-NH$_2$	250	77	3.2
61-425	—	N	-(CH$_2$)$_3$-N(H)CH$_3$	250	2.5	100
AMITRIPTYLINE	-CH$_2$-CH$_2$-	C	=CH·CH$_2$·CH$_2$·N(CH$_3$)$_2$	250	18,181	0.01
NORTRIPTYLINE	-CH$_2$-CH$_2$-	C	=CH·CH$_2$-CH$_2$·N(H)CH$_3$	182	769	0.24
PROTRIPTYLINE	-CH=CH-	-CH-	-(CH$_2$)$_3$-N(H)CH$_3$	167	100	1.7
IMIPRAMINE	-CH$_2$-CH$_2$-	N	-(CH$_2$)$_3$-N(CH$_3$)$_2$	125	1,000	0.1
DOXEPIN	-O-CH$_2$-	C	=CH·CH$_2$·CH$_2$-N(CH$_3$)$_2$	40	1,538	0.03
DESIPRAMINE	-CH$_2$-CH$_2$-	N	-(CH$_2$)$_3$-N(H)CH$_3$	20	20,000	0.001

FIG. 4. Structure: activity relationships of tricyclic agents in inhibiting catecholamine uptake by synaptosomes of norepinephrine neurons of the hypothalamus and dopamine neurons of the corpus striatum. Relative potencies are expressed as in Fig. 3.

What would be especially valuable would be a drug with a very high degree of selectivity for dopamine neurons. Such an agent might be active in potentiating dopamine in the brains of parkinsonian patients, hence an anti-parkinsonian agent. Moreover, such a drug would also be useful in trying to understand what kinds of behavior are mediated by dopamine or norepinephrine neurons in the brain. One of the drugs we screened, 61–425, was 100 times as active in the corpus striatum as in the hypothalamus, representing a rather high degree of selectivity for dopamine neurons (Fig. 4). There is no apparent chemical reason to explain the selectivity. We have not yet begun behavioral studies on the effects of this drug.

BEHAVIORAL STUDIES OF DOPAMINERGIC AND NORADRENERGIC BRAIN FUNCTION

If inhibition of catecholamine uptake is related to the pharmacological actions of amphetamines, the differential ability of d- and l-amphetamine to inhibit uptake by dopamine and norepinephrine neurons should be reflected in differential effects on behavior mediated by dopaminergic or noradrenergic systems. Thus behavior mediated by central norepinephrine should be affected more by d- than by l-amphetamine, while the two isomers should have similar effects on behavior mediated by dopaminergic systems.

Amphetamine produces two characteristic behavioral effects in rats: (1) locomotor stimulation which is thought to reflect the central stimulant properties of this drug in man, and (2) a stereotyped compulsive-gnawing syndrome. There is strong evidence that amphetamine-induced locomotor stimulation involves brain catecholamines. Some authors have attributed this effect to brain norepinephrine,[16,19] while others have assigned the predominant role to dopamine.[18] We compared the effects of *d*- and *l*-amphetamine on locomotor activity of rats measured by a photo-cell recorder. For both *d*- and *l*-isomers, activity was enhanced with increasing doses after which higher doses reduced activity. The time course for amphetamine action was the same for the two isomers. However, *d*-amphetamine was about 10 times as potent as *l*-amphetamine (Fig. 5), a result which parallels the 10-fold difference in ability to inhibit catecholamine uptake by norepinephrine neurons.

There have been many theories to explain the central stimulant action of the amphetamines, including synaptic release of norepinephrine, MAO inhibition, and a direct receptor action. The close parallel between variations in potency of the two amphetamine isomers in inhibiting norepinephrine uptake and enhancing locomotor activity suggests that inhibition of norepinephrine uptake may be a major mechanism of action. It also suggests strongly that brain dopamine, or at least inhibition of its reuptake, is not involved in central stimulant actions of the amphetamines.

The stereotyped behavior seems to be present in many species including humans.[4,10] In rodents the stereotyped behaviors consist predominantly of sniffing, licking, and gnawing. In other species, such as cats and monkeys, there is a considerable element of searching behavior[5] which is manifested in visual seeking activity. It has been suggested that such "searching" behavior is a general effect, and that species variations simply reflect the varying ways that different animals explore their environment. Of practical importance is the ob-

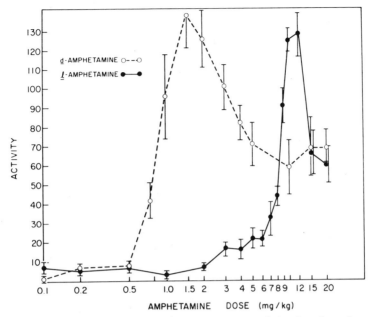

FIG. 5. Enhancement of locomotor activity by *d*- and *l*-amphetamine in rats. Activity was assessed with a photo-cell recorder by recording the number of times that a rat crossed the beam of light during a 30 min session. Rats were placed in their cages 30 min prior to amphetamine administration, and photo-cell recordings were initiated 5 min after amphetamine injection.

servation in monkeys during chronic methamphetamine administration that the stereotyped behavior closely resembles the behavior of human amphetamine addicts, particularly during drug-induced psychosis.[5]

The stereotyped compulsive gnawing behavior produced by amphetamine has been attributed by some workers to stimulation of dopaminergic mechanisms in the corpus striatum, since it is abolished by removal of the corpus striatum.[6,10] Such studies, however, suffer from the criticism that the procedures employed invariably produce profound effects on other brain regions. We compared the ability of d- and l-amphetamine to produce compulsive gnawing in rats. d-Amphetamine was about twice as potent as l-amphetamine (Fig. 6),

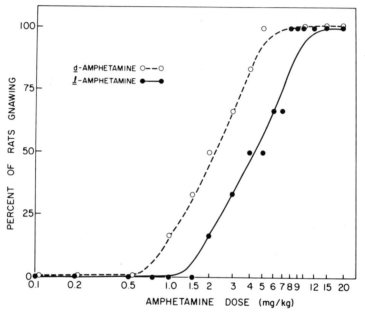

FIG. 6. Production of compulsive gnawing in rats by d- and l-amphetamine. Rats were maintained individually in cages with a wire-grid floor. Compulsive gnawing was considered to be present when rats were gnawing, chewing, or licking the grid floor and, when after lifting the rats from the grid and replacing them, they resumed gnawing within 10 secs.

although this difference was not quite statistically significant. This is far less than the 10-fold difference in the effects of these two isomers on locomotor activity and suggests that a dopaminergic component may be of importance for the compulsive gnawing behavior. However, if inhibition of striatal dopamine uptake were the sole factor in producing gnawing, one might have expected the two isomers to have exactly equal potencies. Perhaps a certain level of noradrenergic stimulation is required to "turn on" the dopaminergic component of gnawing behavior.

TRANYLCYPROMINE ISOMERS: OPPOSITE PATTERNS IN INHIBITING MONOAMINE OXIDASE AND THE CATECHOLAMINE UPTAKE SYSTEM

The great success in deriving potentially valuable clinical information from a simple comparison of the stereoisomers of amphetamine prompted us to explore steric properties of amphetamine-like drugs more closely.

Tranylcypromine, an amphetamine derivative, is a potent inhibitor of MAO and a clinically efficacious antidepressant. Although careful clinical evaluation in double-blind studies has repeatedly confirmed the antidepressant efficacy of tranylcypromine, other MAO inhibitors, particularly isocarboxazid and nialamide, do not appear to be effective antidepressants (Davis, 1965). Still others, such as phenelzine and pargyline, are moderately effective antidepressants, better than isocarboxazid and nialamide but less effective than tranylcypromine.

Since tranylcypromine can inhibit catecholamine reuptake in the peripheral nervous system,[9] we had compared its ability to impair the norepinephrine uptake system in brain with that of other MAO inhibitors.[7] We observed a close correlation between potency in inhibiting the catecholamine uptake system and antidepressant efficacy.[7] Accordingly, we had suggested that all antidepressants, MAO inhibitors as well as the tricyclic agents, might owe their clinical effects, at least in part, to potentiation of synaptically released catecholamines by inhibition of their reuptake inactivation. Recently, Schildkraut[11] noted that tranylcypromine might also release catecholamines. This theory would provide a unitary explanation for the clinical action of antidepressant drugs.

How might one answer the question of whether tranylcypromine and possibly other MAO inhibitors act as antidepressants by interfering with catecholamine reuptake or by inhibiting MAO? Recently (Horn and Snyder, *in preparation*) we have made some observations with isomers of tranylcypromine that might point to a solution. As with amphetamine, there are *d-* and *l-*isomers of tranylcypromine. The *d-* form of the drug is between 5 and 15 times more potent than the *l-* isomer in inhibiting MAO. We compared their potency in inhibiting catecholamine uptake by synaptosomes from the hypothalamus or striatum of the rat (Table 2). Strikingly, the *l-*isomer was three times more potent than *d-*tranylcypromine in inhibiting catecholamine uptake by hypothalamic synaptosomes and twice as potent in the corpus striatum.

These findings suggest that, if MAO inhibition is responsible for the antidepressant activity, *d-*tranylcypromine should be the more active agent, while if inhibition of catecholamine uptake is crucial, the *l-*isomer should be more potent. There are several animal models to evaluate the activity of antidepressants, such as

TABLE 2. *Relative potency of tranylcypromine isomers in blocking catecholamine uptake into the hypothalamus and corpus striatum*

	ID_{50}	
	Hypothalamus	Striatum
d-*trans*-2-phenylcyclopropylamine	$1.0 - 1.5 \times 10^{-6}$	$3.6 - 4.0 \times 10^{-6}$
l-*trans*-2-phenylcyclopropylamine	$4.5 - 6.5 \times 10^{-7}$	$1.0 - 1.2 \times 10^{-7}$

Each ID_{50} determination was carried out with three concentrations of inhibitor in quadruplicate. Values presented are the mean obtained in three to four determinations. The lower ID_{50} value for the *l*-isomer in both regions indicates its greater potency in inhibiting catecholamine uptake.

reversal of reserpine-induced sedation, which might be good test systems for ascertaining the mechanism of tranylcypromine's antidepressant activity. Currently such behavioral evaluation is in progress in our laboratory.

If *l*-tranylcypromine were the more active antidepressant, this would have important therapeutic implications. The most serious side-effects of tranylcypromine stem from its MAO inhibitory activity. These adverse effects, including hyperpyrexia and hypertensive crises, were sufficiently serious that for a period of time tranylcypromine was withdrawn from the market. Use of *l*-tranylcypromine, which is about one-tenth as effective an inhibitor of MAO as the *d*-isomer, might greatly reduce the risk of the dangerous side-effects that stem from MAO inhibition.

ACKNOWLEDGMENTS

This investigation was supported by U.S. Public Health Service grants MH–18501, NS–07275, and GM–16492. S.H.S. is the recipient of NIMH Research

Scientist Development Award MH–33128. A.S.H. is the recipient of a Wellcome Trust Foundation travel grant.

REFERENCES

1. Coyle, J. T., and Snyder, S. H. (1969): Catecholamine uptake by synaptosomes in homogenates of rat brain: stereospecificity in different areas. *J. Pharm. Exptl. Ther.*, 170: 221–231.

2. Coyle, J. T., and Snyder, S. H. (1969): Antiparkinsonian drugs: Inhibition of dopamine uptake in the corpus striatum as a possible mechanism of action. *Science,* 166:899–901.

3. Davis, J. M. (1965): The efficacy of the tranquilizing and antidepressant drugs. *Arch. Gen. Psychiat.,* 13:552–572.

4. Ellinwood, E. H., Jr. (1967): Amphetamine psychosis. I. Descriptions of the individual and process. *J. Nerv. Ment. Dis.,* 44:273–280.

5. Ellinwood, E. H., Jr., and Escalanti, O. (1970): Behavior and histopathological findings during chronic methedrine intoxication. *Bio. Psychiat.* 2:27–39.

6. Ernst, A. M. (1967): Mode of action of apomorphine and dexamphetamine on gnawing compulsion in rats. *Psychopharmacologia,* 10:316–323.

7. Hendley, E. D., and Snyder, S. H. (1968): Relationship between the action of monoamine oxidase inhibitors on the noradrenaline uptake system and their antidepressant efficacy. *Nature,* 220:1330–1331.

8. Horn, A. S., Coyle, J. T., and Snyder, S. H. (1971): Catechol-

amine uptake by synaptosomes from rat brain: structure: Activity relationships of drugs with differential effects on dopamine and norepinephrine neurons. *Mol. Pharmacol.*, 7:66–80.

9. Iversen, L. L. (1967): *The Uptake and Storage of Noradrenaline in Sympathetic Nerves.* Cambridge University Press, New York.

10. Randrup, A., and Munkvad, I. (1967): Stereotyped activities produced by amphetamine in several animal species and man. *Psychopharmacologia*, 11:300–310.

11. Schildkraut, J. (1970): Tranylcypromine: Effects on norepinephrine metabolism in rat brain. *Amer. J. Psychiat.*, 126: 925–932.

12. Snyder, S. H. (1970): Putative neurotransmitters in the brain: Selective neuronal uptake, subcellular localization, and interactions with centrally acting drugs. *Biological Psychiatry*, 2:367–389.

13. Snyder, S. H., and Coyle, J. T. (1969): Regional differences in ^{3}H-norepinephrine and ^{3}H-dopamine uptake into rat brain homogenates. *J. Pharm. Exptl. Ther.*, 165:78–86.

14. Snyder, S. H., Kuhar, M. J., Green, A. I., Coyle, J. T., and Shaskan, E. G. (1970a): Uptake and subcellular localization of neurotransmitters in the brain. *Int. Rev. Neurobiol.*, 13:127–158.

15. Snyder, S. H., Taylor, K. M., Coyle, J. T., and Meyerhoff, J. L. (1970b): The role of brain dopamine in behavioral regulation and the actions of psychotropic drugs. *Amer. J. Psychiat.*, 127:117–207.

16. Sulser, F., Owens, M. L., Norvich, M. R., and Dingell, J. V. (1968): The relative role of storage and synthesis of brain norepinephrine in the psychomotor stimulation evoked by amphetamine or by desipramine and tetrabenazine. *Psychopharmacologia,* 12:322–332.

17. Taylor, K. M., and Snyder, S. H. (1970): Amphetamine: Differentiation by *d*- and *l*-isomers of behavior involving brain norepinephrine or dopamine. *Science,* 168:1487–1489.

18. Van Rossum, J. M., Van der Schoot, J. B., and Hurkamns, J. A. Thm. M. (1962): Mechanism of action of cocaine and amphetamine in the brain. *Experientia,* 18:229–231.

19. Weissman, A., Koe, B. K., and Tenen, S. S. (1966): Antiamphetamine effects following inhibition of tyrosine hydroxylase. *J. Pharm. Exptl. Ther.* 151:339–352.

Behavioral Abnormalities Occurring in Parkinsonism During Treatment with L-DOPA

Roger C. Duvoisin and Melvin D. Yahr

A total of 283 patients with Parkinson's disease were admitted to a clinical investigation of L-DOPA conducted at the Columbia-Presbyterian Medical Center in New York City from December 1967 through June 1969. Abnormalities of behavior which were observed in this large group of patients on long-term treatment with L-DOPA will be described in this chapter. The methods of treatment, evaluation, and patient selection and the results observed in the initial patients of this group have been previously described.[1,2] Nearly all the patients (270) had classical Parkinson's disease at various stages of its progression ranging from mild non-disabling disease to far advanced disease with complete invalidism. In addition there were eight patients with a definite diagnosis of post-encephalitic parkinsonism established according to criteria we have previously defined,[3] one patient with parkinsonism secondary to brain tumor, two presenting an atypical parkinsonian syndrome believed to represent progressive supra-

nuclear palsy, and two patients with atypical parkinsonism of undetermined cause.

Previous occurrences of behavioral disorders in the
present patient group are summarized in Table 1. Fifty
patients had experienced clinically overt toxic psychic
reactions on their previous drug therapy which had
cleared on withdrawal of the offending drug or reduction
of its dosage prior to the institution of L-DOPA therapy.
Seventeen patients had been sufficiently depressed to
require specific treatment; fifteen of these patients were
still chronically depressed when they began treatment
with L-DOPA. Two patients had made previous suicide
attempts but neither was overtly depressed at the time
of admission to the L-DOPA study. Five patients had
a history of functional psychosis which had previously
required psychiatric hospitalization. Few details were
available regarding these previous episodes. One of
these five patients had received psychotherapy for
several years for "chronic paranoia." An additional
patient had presented mild paranoid delusions and can-
cerophobia for many years but had never required specific therapeutic measures. Finally, nineteen patients
were accepted for treatment who had significant chronic
brain syndromes ranging in severity from mild senility
to severe dementia.

In the initial phases of the L-DOPA program, an
effort was made to withdraw all previous treatment in
every patient prior to commencing treatment with
L-DOPA. Later, however, previous drugs were often
continued usually at a reduced dosage because they pro-
vided some degree of protection against the side effects of L-DOPA and because many patients derived
some benefit from their continued use as adjuncts to

TABLE 1. *Previous mental disorders in 283 parkinson patients accepted for treatment with L-DOPA*

Previous disorder	Number
toxic psychic reactions provoked by standard anti-parkinsonian drugs	50
depression	17
suicide attempts	2
chronic brain syndrome	19
functional psychosis	5
total	93

L-DOPA. Thus 185 (approximately 65%) of the patients under discussion continued on some anticholinergic anti-parkinson drug such as trihexyphenidyl (Artane®) or diphenhydramine (Benadryl®) through all or most of the trial period. There were several instances of toxic reactions provoked by these anticholinergic drugs which occurred when their dosage was increased and cleared when their dosage was decreased. These reactions are specially excluded from the present analysis. Patients with pre-existing disorders which persisted unchanged on L-DOPA therapy are also excluded.

GENERAL OBSERVATIONS

In our initial reports on L-DOPA therapy, we described a number of psychic effects of the drug we had observed which may probably be regarded as normal and which were on the whole desirable. There was a general alerting, frequently noted as one of the first beneficial effects shortly after commencing L-DOPA therapy.

A mild euphoria was also frequently seen which was thought to reflect the patient's reaction to their clinical improvement in motor function. An increase of dreaming was often reported by our patients. Some described a return of normal dreams for the first time in many years.

In many patients there was an apparent improvement in mental function. It is difficult to say to what extent such improvement reflected the withdrawal or reduction of dosage of centrally active anticholinergic drugs, but we have retained our initial impression of some mild but definite improvement in many patients. In the initial stages of treatment with L-DOPA, patients frequently showed an increased interest in their surroundings and greater participation in social activities in the hospital and at home. Renewed interest in family and sometimes business affairs was noted in parallel with a general increase in the spontaneity of intellectual as well as motor activity. In short, there seemed to be at least a partial reversal of the mental changes characteristic of Parkinson's disease.

An increase in sexual activity was reported by a small but significant proportion of the patients or their spouses. A systematic survey was not undertaken so that the true incidence of this phenomenon cannot be assessed from the present data. However, it seems noteworthy that 8% of our patients reported an increase of sexual activity. Generally, this appeared to us to represent a partial return toward normalcy. Complaints from spouses regarding increased libido in our patients seemed to reflect sexual maladjustments which had been masked by the motor disability of Parkinson's disease and were now unmasked by the general improvement brought about by L-DOPA treatment. Hypersexuality was encountered only in senile dements or as a feature of a more generalized disturbance, e.g., hypomanic behavior. A true aphrodisiac effect was thus not observed.

Families who at first were grateful for the patient's restoration to a more normal life sometimes complained later on that the patient became too stubborn or independent, too impatient, aggressive or even unruly. Such complaints did not necessarily reflect abnormal behavior but rather conflicts arising as a consequence of rapid changes in the patient's functional capacity. The numerous adjustments which some families had gradually made in response to a patient's progressive disabilities over periods of many years were suddenly destroyed when a chronically invalid parkinsonian improved sufficiently to attempt to regain an active role in family affairs and reclaim long-lost prerogatives and authority. Such "disturbances," however, seemed to us a measure of L-DOPA's therapeutic efficacy rather than evidence of psychotoxicity, and were not counted as behavioral abnormalities. They do, however, deserve mention as a significant clinical problem which should be anticipated and which may require positive action.

BEHAVIORAL DISTURBANCES

Significant behavioral disturbances were encountered in 73 (25.8%) of our 283 patients. The number affected in each age range and the age structure of our patient population are shown in Table 2. The types of behavioral disturbances observed and the number of patients affected are shown in Table 3. The patients were grouped according to their predominant clinical feature.

TABLE 2. *Behavioral disturbances in parkinson patients during L-DOPA treatment*

Age	No. patients	No. disturbed
30's	1	1
40's	25	9
50's	82	21
60's	124	30
70's	46	11
80's	5	1
	283	73 (26%)

TABLE 3. *Behavioral disturbances observed in 283 patients on L-DOPA therapy*

Disturbance	No. patients
agitation	23
confusion	21
hypomanic behavior	7
depression	6
acute psychosis	6
illusions/hallucinations	7
attempted suicide	3
total	73

Agitation, the most frequent disturbance, appeared to represent an exaggeration of the normal and desirable effects of L-DOPA described above. Correction of the loss of spontaneity and emotional reactivity so characteristic of parkinsonism progressed in some patients beyond a desirable level to frank restlessness and agitation. Periods of agitation were usually brief. They developed and subsided in a temporal pattern related to the dosage schedule, paralleling the appearance of choreiform involuntary movements, and reaching a peak 2 to 3 hours after each dose so that a broad spectrum of behavioral changes could be seen in the same patient in a period of just a few hours. In most patients these undesirable side effects diminished when the dosage was reduced and their intensity could be "titrated" by varying the dose.

Agitation precluded effective dosage of L-DOPA in 10 patients, 6 of whom were discontinued for this reason. However, minor degrees of nervousness or "inner agitation" tended also to diminish in time, subsiding after several months of continuing L-DOPA treatment even without a dosage reduction. To a considerable extent, the frequency and severity of these symptoms reflected the manner in which the patients were treated, the aggressiveness with which the L-DOPA dosage was increased during the initial periods of treatment, and the ability of the treating physician to recognize them in their incipient stages and respond with dosage adjustments and other therapeutic measures.

In a small number of patients, agitation and hyperactivity were associated with impulsive, aggressive, and inappropriate behavior in a pattern reminiscent of the hypomanic phase of manic-depressive psychosis. This behavior was often episodic, exhibiting a diurnal variation related to the dosage schedule and accompanied by choreiform movements.

Periods of confusion, usually mild and transient, were noted in 21 patients. In eight, confusion was associated with illusions and/or hallucinations. One patient had only a single severe episode in the initial period of treatment which subsided without a change in treatment. In four patients there was a clear correlation between the occurrences of confusion and the dose of L-DOPA. Five patients experienced less confusion on L-DOPA than on their previous treatment. Twelve patients were receiving a conventional anti-parkinsonian drug as an adjunct to L-DOPA but were retained in this tabulation because they had not exhibited confusion previously on these agents at equivalent or even greater dosages.

Chronic depression was noted in 15 patients at the time they began treatment with L-DOPA. In four of these patients, symptoms of depression appeared to diminish or disappear, and in one patient they increased appreciably; in the majority there was no appreciable change. Three of the patients who remained depressed attempted suicide; one attempt was successful. These three patients had been greatly disappointed that L-DOPA had failed to alter their circumstances or to relieve a particularly disturbing symptom or disability. Depression developed *de novo* in the course of long-term treatment in six patients who had been on continuous L-DOPA treatment for 1 year or more and had responded poorly to L-DOPA or at least less well than had been hoped.

An acute toxic psychosis occurred in only six patients in the course of the trial. In four patients, the psychotic episodes were fairly typical of drug-induced delirium; in the other two patients, they were more typical of acute paranoid schizophrenia with well-systematized delusions, auditory hallucinations, and paranoid thinking. These two patients had previously been under psychiatric care for functional psychosis requiring institutional care, one with a diagnosis of paranoid schizophrenia and the other with a diagnosis of chronic paranoia. Thus, while it appears that latent schizophrenia may have been activated in these two patients, it should be noted that situational stresses were operative in one of them, that both episodes occurred after a long period of treatment at a stable dose, and moreover that two of the four patients in this group whose reactions resembled drug delirium also had a history of previous functional psychosis. It also seems worthy of note that three of the six patients who developed acute psychotic reactions on L-DOPA had had previous psychoses provoked by anti-cholinergic anti-parkinsonian drugs. These data are summarized in Table 4.

TABLE 4.   *Analysis of six patients who had an acute toxic psychosis on L-DOPA therapy*

	Previous history		L-DOPA therapy		
Patient	Functional psychosis	Drug delirium	Functional psychosis	Drug delirium	Treatment stopped
6	+	+		+	−
88	+	−	+	−	+
189	−	+	−	+	−
193	+	−	−	+	−
018	−	+	−	+	−
060	+	−	+	−	+

Hallucinatory phenomena were noted in 15 patients in addition to the 6 described above who had acute psychotic episodes. Usually these were visual hallucinations recognized as unreal by the patients at least some of the time. Six of the patients exhibited no obvious features suggestive either of psychosis or an organic mental syndrome and appeared to be mentally normal on clinical examination of their mental status. Eight patients experiencing hallucinations, however, were among the 17 patients with pre-existing organic mental syndromes admitted to the study. Visual hallucinations had occurred in these eight patients on their previous anticholinergic therapy; in four of these, the hallucinatory phenomena were less severe on L-DOPA than they had been on their previous therapy; in three the hallucinations were greater in L-DOPA.

CORRELATION WITH PREVIOUS DISTURBANCES

Only 14 of the 50 patients who had previously experienced toxic psychic effects while taking anticholinergic anti-parkinsonian agents developed behavioral disturbances while on L-DOPA. This proportion is similar to the overall incidence of behavioral disturbances in the entire population of 283 patients. Analysis of the types of disturbances observed in these 14 patients revealed little correspondence between the behavioral disturbances associated with L-DOPA and those associated with previous anticholinergic drug therapy. In five patients, the disturbances associated with L-DOPA were milder than those previously provoked by the anticholinergic drugs.

Nine of the 19 patients with chronic brain syndromes developed significant behavioral disturbances on L-DOPA therapy. All 19 had previously had disturbances on anticholinergic drugs. It may be noted that eight of these 19 patients derived significant therapeutic benefit from L-DOPA, and only four patients failed to show useful improvement at tolerable doses.

Four of the five patients with a history of previous functional psychosis had behavioral disorders, and in two of these the disorder appeared to be a recurrence of their previous psychosis.

COMMENT

It may be argued that the population of patients described was deliberately selected to exclude patients with major behavioral disorders which it was feared might be exacerbated by L-DOPA or which might render the evaluation of therapeutic responses and side effects difficult as is proper in the initial clinical investigation of an experimental therapeutic agent, and that consequently our experience may fail to predict adequately the incidence and severity of the complications which will be encountered when L-DOPA is employed in the parkinson population at large. On the other hand, it may be noted that in an effort to include all disturbances which might have been L-DOPA-induced, we retained in our analysis some patients in whom the relationship of behavioral disturbances to L-DOPA therapy was probably merely coincidental. In several patients, for example, it appeared quite possible that a change of behavior was a reaction to circumstances rather than an untoward drug effect. The six patients who became depressed after being on L-DOPA therapy for some period of time were disappointed by the failure of L-DOPA to alter their circumstances sufficiently. The three patients who attempted suicide did so after concluding that L-DOPA would not relieve a particularly disturbing symptom or disability. We have the impression that they then proceeded with previously formulated suicide plans. A similar interpretation has been made by other observers.[4] It is thus doubtful that depression can truly be considered a side effect of L-DOPA. In some demented patients, it seemed clear that abnormal behavior merely reflected the improved motor function which enabled them to act upon their illusions and hallucinations more readily. For these several reasons, we have probably overestimated the incidence of behavioral disorders which may be ascribed to L-DOPA. We conclude that on balance our experience does closely predict the type and incidence of behavioral disturbances which may be observed in parkinson patients on L-DOPA therapy, leaving aside the question of the etiologic role of L-DOPA in these disturbances.

In general, it may be said that behavioral disturbances associated with L-DOPA resemble those produced by amphetamines. The most frequent phenomena are agitation, restlessness, and aggressive, impulsive behavior sometimes bordering on hypomania. Less common was confusion usually occurring in brief transient episodes. Acute delirium was uncommon and, in any case, nonspecific.

Patients with a chronic brain syndrome are more likely to develop behavioral disturbances on L-DOPA therapy than are other patients. Moreover, they may not be able to benefit in a meaningful way from otherwise significant improvement in motor function resulting from L-DOPA therapy. Nevertheless, dementia need not preclude the use of L-DOPA, and some demented patients appear to tolerate L-DOPA better than they do the anticholinergic drugs.

The implication that L-DOPA may activate a latent schizophrenia must be taken seriously; however, it should be noted that the differentiation of acute delirium from schizophrenia may be quite difficult since delusional ideation with paranoid features may persist for some time after cognitive disturbances have subsided or even in some cases in their absence. Granting that there probably is a significant risk, it remains uncertain whether this risk is greater with L-DOPA than with other drugs or intoxicants, and it would be premature to conclude that the use of L-DOPA is absolutely contraindicated in patients with a previous history of schizophrenia. Certainly, some patients with such a history or even with continuing psychopathology may tolerate L-DOPA satisfactorily and derive valuable improvement in motor function.

L-DOPA does not offer much promise for the alleviation of depression in parkinsonian patients. Although specific documentation was not obtained, it does seem that dibenzepine drugs (amitriptyline and imipramine) were effective in patients on L-DOPA therapy and that their effect may have been augmented.

Some parkinson patients on L-DOPA do experience increased libido which probably represents a return toward normalcy. Possibly, this improvement may reflect the withdrawal of anticholinergic drugs. It has been suggested that loss of libido may be an intrinsic feature of Parkinson's disease which may be at least partially corrected by L-DOPA.[5] The complexities of the subject make a definitive judgment unwarranted at this time.

It seems pertinent to compare the psychotoxicity of L-DOPA with that of the anticholinergic drugs which are commonly employed in treating parkinsonism. The toxic psychic efforts produced by the latter have not been adequately appreciated. They are the single most important dose-limiting side effect of these drugs and occur to some degree in most if not all patients receiving clinically effective dosages. It may be noted that 16% of the present trial population gave a history of previous psychotoxicity due to anticholinergic drugs. The actual incidence was probably somewhat higher. In a statistical survey of a large number of parkinson patients carried out the year prior to the beginning of the L-DOPA investigation and involving a comparable population, the overall incidence of overt clinically significant mental and behavioral disturbances was 19.8% (R. C. Duvoisin and R. B. Barrett, *unpublished data*). The age structure of that patient population and the incidence of disturbances in each age range are shown in Table 5. It appears that L-DOPA does not produce significantly more mental disturbances than do the anticholinergic antiparkinson drugs, at least during the early phases of treatment and within the time limits of the present study.

TABLE 5. *Behavioral disturbances in parkinson patients provoked by anticholinergic drugs*

Age	No. patients	No. disturbed
30's	3	—
40's	18	2
50's	63	7
60's	113	24
70's	47	14
80's	3	2
total	247	49 (19.8%)

The behavioral disorders provoked by the anticholinergic drugs differed from those we ascribed to L-DOPA in several respects. There was a striking correlation of toxicity with age which was not evident with L-DOPA, the incidence of mental disturbance being much lower under age 60 with the anticholinergic drugs. The cognitive dysfunction so characteristic of the former were milder and much less frequent with L-DOPA. Indeed, L-DOPA tended typically to produce agitation and excitement reminiscent of amphetamine intoxication. Finally, patients who had experienced disturbances with anticholinergic drugs were not more likely than others to be disturbed by L-DOPA. These considerations suggest that different central mechanisms are involved in the psychotoxicity of the two classes of drugs. In fact, it is our impression that mental disturbances related to L-DOPA are less severe if not less frequent than those associated with anticholinergic drugs. We conclude that in regard to mental side effects, as in other aspects, L-DOPA represents a significant advance over the previous anticholinergic drug therapy.

REFERENCES

1. Duvoisin, R., Barrett, R., Schear, M. et al. (1969): The use of L-DOPA in parkinsonism. In: Third Symposium on Parkinson's Disease, edited by F. J. Gillingham and I. M. Donaldson, 185–191. E. & S. Livingstone Ltd., Edinburgh.

2. Yahr, M. D., Duvoisin, R. C., and Schear, M. (1969): Treatment of parkinsonism with levo-DOPA. *Archives of Neurology*, 21:343.

3. Duvoisin, R. C., and Yahr, M. D. (1965): Encephalitis and parkinsonism. *Archives of Neurology*, 12:227.

4. Celesia, G. C., and Barr, A. N. (1970): Psychosis and other psychiatric manifestations of levo-DOPA. *Archives of Neurology*, 23:193.

5. Constantinidis, J., and Ajuriaguerra, J. de (1970): Syndrome familial ave tremblement Parkinsonien et anosmie et sa therapeutique par la L-DOPA. . . . *Therapeutique,* 46:263.

L-DOPA Treatment of Impotence: A Clinical and Experimental Study

O. Benkert

CLINICAL STUDY

A return of sexual potency was occasionally observed after treating parkinsonian patients with L-DOPA. The question was asked if the increase in potency was really due to L-DOPA treatment or if it was only a return toward the normal condition of those patients who for years had suffered from this condition. Before the question could be answered, we studied just how much L-DOPA could actually influence the potency of otherwise healthy patients.

We tried in a pilot study to ascertain the effect of L-DOPA on ten male patients whose impotence was primarily organic. These were out-patients who sought medical advice and who complained either of insufficient penile erection ability or of insufficient penile erection combined with decreased libido. Patients chosen for our pilot study were impotent for at least one year and were at least 25 years of age with enough sexual intercourse experience. Psychic factors, especially partner rejection, were excluded. Nine out of ten patients had permanent partners. Six of these ten patients had undergone an unsuccessful testosterone treatment for several weeks before the L-DOPA treatment.

Tape recordings were taken during interviews with a psychiatrist before and after various treatment periods, and then evaluated by two other doctors.

Four patients received L-DOPA combined with the decarboxylase inhibitor Ro 4–4602 (N-(D,L-seryl)-N¹-(2,3,4-trihydroxybenzyl)-hydrazine HCl) for a 3-week period, which was gradually increased to a dosage of 200 mg Ro 4–4602 and 800 mg L-DOPA per day. After that, these four patients received only 5 g per day of L-DOPA (the other patients received this dosage at the start). After this, L-DOPA dosage intake of 5 g per day for 10 days, a 3 g per day L-DOPA dosage was given for approximately another 10 weeks.

The usual laboratory tests were followed continuously. Pathological findings were not established; three patients had diabetes mellitus, but we found no L-DOPA influence on blood-sugar levels. The pulse frequency slowly increased with L-DOPA alone, but did not become pathological. Blood pressure usually decreased slightly in the beginning. Hyperkinesia was not observed. Psychic changes were not found.

We started with 10 patients. One patient had to be eliminated after 4 weeks because of irritability, and another one because of collapse after an intake of 1.5 g L-DOPA during the second week. After a period of 12 weeks, the treatment was terminated. Seven of 9 patients who received L-DOPA for at least 4 weeks showed a small increase in penile erection after 2 to 4 weeks; of these seven patients, one observed a big increase and was very optimistic. However, after 6 to 8 weeks, penile erection decreased again and returned to its former state, even though a 3-g L-DOPA dosage was given. Only one patient was successful after 12 weeks. But not one patient had satisfactory sexual intercourse even though penile erection had increased. Complete penile erection was also lacking during L-DOPA intake. After 3 weeks it was noticed by four patients that spontaneous erection appeared more frequently in the mornings, and still more frequently by two of these four patients after 6 and 10 weeks, respectively. One of these patients also showed increased erection during the day. Three patients informed us of a changed consistency and volume of ejaculation. Two of these patients found that the consistency was more liquid before L-DOPA intake; after a 3-week L-DOPA intake, the consistency resembled gelatin. Two patients noticed a considerable volume increase. One patient felt pain in the testis and spermatic cord; furthermore, the interruption of urination was not possible before treatment, but was possible during L-DOPA intake. Another patient reported that his urine contained sperm in the morning.

Increased libido was noticed by two patients after 2 to 4 weeks, but after 12 weeks only one patient showed a distinct increase. This patient had also experienced more sexual fantasies during the day; another experienced more sexual dreams during the night.

Six patients showed increased working capacity. Two of these patients needed less sleep, but one patient became extremely nervous and highly irritable so that — as mentioned above — L-DOPA had to be discontinued. However, working capacity decreased after 12 weeks of L-DOPA treatment.

To summarize, one can draw the following conclusions from these findings.

No change had been noticed after three weeks of decarboxylase inhibitor plus L-DOPA; only after administration of L-DOPA alone was at least a slight increase of penile erection observed, as well as more frequent spontaneous erections in the mornings. Nevertheless, increase of penile erection did not lead to satisfactory sexual intercourse. Also, physical symptoms in the genital area seemed to be noticed. Libido was increased in only two patients. The initial L-DOPA effect disappeared again after a lengthy L-DOPA intake. There was no difference between 5-g and 3-g doses. The increased working capacity declined again after lengthy L-DOPA intake.

Even though L-DOPA therapy on the whole does not show the desired effect upon organic impotence, nevertheless, a slight effect in the genital area cannot be overlooked.

To return to the initial question: Does L-DOPA specifically increase potency in parkinsonism? We believe we can state from these preliminary results that L-DOPA alone is not able to increase potency significantly. The increased potency in parkinsonian patients treated with L-DOPA is most likely traced back to the improvement of their general well-being.

EXPERIMENTAL STUDY

How does L-DOPA influence the sexual behavior of animals? We have included the mounting behavior between male rats as a criterion for sexual behavior in our experiments, but we are aware of the problem in balancing the mounting behavior inducement and heterosexual activation. We tried to ascertain if a relationship existed between increased mounting behavior and a specific amount of biogenic amines in the brain of rats.

L-DOPA alone does not lead to mounting behavior in rats, with either high or low dosages. After the combination of Ro 4–4602 plus L-DOPA, only one out of forty rats showed mounting behavior, which in comparison to other groups must be considered negative (Table 1). Observations followed 1 hr after the L-DOPA injection of four rats in each cage. Ro 4–4602 (50 mg/kg) was injected 45 min before L-DOPA (200 mg/kg). The combination of Ro 4–4602 plus L-DOPA leads to a high and significant increase in dopamine (DA), to a slight but insignificant increase of 7% in norepinephrine (NE), and a significant decrease of 41.1% in serotonin (5-HT) in the brain. When the DA level is further increased and the 5-HT level is decreased to 34.2% by pretreatment with reserpine, it caused mounting behavior in one of four rats (1/4) (3 up to 40 mountings in the observed time) in almost every cage.

When a para-chlorophenylalanine (PCPA) pretreatment instead of reserpine was given, it caused a considerable increase in mounting behavior. In almost every cage, two out of four rats showed mountings. This was especially noticeable in those animals which had manifested an increase in mounting behavior when treated only with PCPA the evening before. PCPA alone did not lead to increased mounting behavior during the time of our observations between 9 A.M. and noon. When PCPA is combined with Ro 4–4602 plus L-DOPA, the relationship between a high DA level and a low 5-HT level remains. NE in the brain does not seem to be of any decisive importance in inducing mounting behavior.

TABLE 1. Correlation between brain amine level and behavior

Substance, i.p. (mg/kg)				Brain levels (%)			Behavior	
Reserpine	PCPA	Ro 4-4602	L-DOPA	DA	NE	5-HT	Mountings	Fights
–	–	50	200	740.0 ± 23	107.0 ± 7	41.1 ± 3	0	+
2	–	50	200	1,050.0 ± 40	60.9 ± 5	34.2 ± 2	+	++
–	3 × 100	50	200	532.0 ± 15	105.5 ± 6	38.5 ± 2	++	++

The amine level of the whole brain was listed in % of controls. The controls were injected with saline. DA = 1.07 ± 0.116 mg/kg; NE = 0.45 ± 0.046 mg/kg; 5-HT = 0.83 ± 0.098. Each value refers to 4 to 10 rats. Reserpine was injected 16 hr, and Ro 4–4602 45 min before L-DOPA. PCPA was injected three times at 24-hr intervals; 24 hr after the last PCPA injection, Ro 4–4602 plus L-DOPA was given. The time of observation follows 1 hr after the L-DOPA injection for 4 rats in each cage (4 to 10 cages).

The note 1/4—4/4 refers to the number of active animals in a cage (max. 4/4); the symbols (rarely, often, very often) relate to the number of cages in which the respective behavior was observed.

Mountings:	+: often 1/4; 3 to 40 mountings
	++: very often 2/4; 3 to 40 mountings
Fights:	+: rarely 2/4; < 5 fights
	++: often 2/4, sometimes 3/4 or 4/4; 5 to 20 fights
	+++: very often 2/4–4/4; > 20 fights

The mounting behavior seems to be caused by a lowered 5-HT and an increased DA level in the brain. It is important to note that fighting behavior increased along with mounting behavior. We realize, of course, that the state of metabolism in the nerve endings can be described only to a limited extent by the brain amine concentration alone.

We are planning to try out the results of this animal model (increase of DA and decrease of 5-HT in the brain) on man together with hormone therapy.

L-DOPA Treatment of Depression

N. Matussek

We tested the acute effect of L-DOPA upon depression in our preliminary experiments with intravenous injections of 25 to 50 mg L-DOPA[12] and followed
up with a dose of up to 100 mg per day (*unpublished
results*). We chose this dosage after the experience of
Birkmayer and Hornykiewicz[3] in the treatment of parkinsonism. These authors found a distinct influence
upon akinesia and rigor, especially in the lesser cases of
parkinsonism, shortly after an intravenous injection.
We must therefore assume that, even with these small
L-DOPA dosages, enough dopamine was formed in the
CNS.

We conducted these and later experiments only on
patients where retardation stood in the foreground of
depression. Psychostimulating effects were noted in
eight out of ten experiments with 25 to 50 mg and in
three out of thirteen experiments with 100 mg i.v.
L-DOPA.

In order to recheck these results, we carried out a
double-blind study in which we administered orally
150 mg L-DOPA combined with 300 mg decarboxylase
inhibitor Ro 4–4602.[11] Again this dosage was chosen
after the results which Birkmayer and Mentasi[4] had col-

lected with this combination in treating parkinsonism. Since this dosage had shown clear therapeutic effects on akinesia and rigor, it is our opinion that at least enough dopamine is formed in the brain.

These examinations were carried out on 31 retarded depressed patients. Eighteen of these patients were treated with DOPA plus Ro 4–4602, and the remaining thirteen patients with placebo, each for a period of 11 to 18 days. (For more experimental details, refer to Matussek et al.[10,11])

Table 1 shows the results of this study. According to the self-rating scale, the improved patients in the DOPA plus Ro 4–4602 group showed that only four patients had improved so much that they could be dis-

TABLE 1. *Influence of Ro 4–4602 and L-DOPA on the self-rating scale*

Drug	I Initial value	II Improved	III Impaired	IV No change
Ro 4–4602 + L-DOPA (18)	30.9	+9.75 (12)	−2.3 (4)	2
Placebo (13)	27.1	+7.3 (5)	−6.2 (6)	2

The average scores of the self-rating scale of both groups before initiation of medication are shown in column I. Columns II, III and IV show the average difference in the scores before beginning the medication and after 11 to 18 days of medication. The numbers show by how many points the condition has improved according to the self-rating scale (column II) or has become impaired (column III), or in how many patients the condition has remained the same (column IV). The number of patients is indicated in parentheses.

charged. The remaining patients in this particular group showed only slight improvement. In the placebo group, only one patient received a score equal to the norm and was discharged.

We had expected an increase of psychomotor activity in our patients under treatment with DOPA plus Ro 4–4602. This expectation was confirmed by the observations of two doctors.

We considered an unsuccessful suicide attempt by one of the patients as an increase in psychomotor activation without an improvement of mood under medication. These observations correspond to the results of Goodwin et al.[7,8], who found an increase in anger and hypomania in some patients without an improvement of their mood.

Our results show that some patients showed an improvement with DOPA plus Ro 4–4602, but in our opinion DOPA is not as suitable for the therapy of retarded depression as for the treatment of parkinsonism. Based on these and other clinical examinations,[6,7,8] the question arises whether the catecholamine or the norepinephrine hypothesis of depression[5,9,13] can still be maintained.

On the basis of our experimental animal biochemical examinations regarding the effect[1,2] of DOPA plus Ro 4–4602, we can make the following conclusions.

(1) Without monoamine oxidase inhibition, it is impossible to bring about a noteworthy increase in norepinephrine similar to the dopamine increase in the brain solely by administering DOPA plus Ro 4–4602 or by high DOPA dosages.

(2) This is probably caused by a deficient metabolism of dopamine to norepinephrine in the brain, since

Vogel et al.[14] showed that a lower dopamine-β-hydroxylase activity than tyrosine-hydroxylase activity is found in the rat brain.

It is, therefore, our opinion that in clinical experiments up to now, with a high DOPA dosage or with the combination of DOPA with a peripheral decarboxylase inhibitor, the norepinephrine concentration in the brain is not elevated to a degree worth mentioning. We also have great doubts, based on our results, that with an almost constant norepinephrine level the norepinephrine turnover in the brain is increased substantially by this treatment.

On the basis of these clinical results of DOPA therapy upon depressive patients, it is our opinion that no conclusions can be drawn regarding a possible norepinephrine deficit in depression. A dopamine deficit in the brain can well be compensated for with DOPA. Even if norepinephrine deficiency is responsible for certain symptoms of depression, DOPA does not appear suitable to compensate for such a deficit.

REFERENCES

1. Benkert, O., Gluba, H., and Matussek, N. (1971a). *Neuropharmacol.* (*in press*).

2. Benkert, O., Renz, A., and Matussek, N. (1971b). *Neuropharmacol.* (*in press*).

3. Birkmayer, W., and Hornykiewicz, O. (1962). *Arch. Psychiat. Nervenkr.,* 203:560.

4. Birkmayer, W., and Mentasi (1967). *Arch. Psych. Zeitschr. Ges. Neurol.,* 210:29.

5. Bunney, W. E., Jr., and Davis, J. M. (1965). *Arch. Gen. Psychiat.*, 13:483.

6. Bunney, W. E., Jr., Murphy, D. L., and Goodwin, F. K. (1970). *Lancet* I, 1022.

7. Goodwin, F. K., Brodie, H. K. H., Murphy, D. L., and Bunney, W. E., Jr. (1970*a*). *Lancet* I, 908.

8. Goodwin, F. K., Brodie, H. K. H., Murphy, D. L., and Bunney, W. E., Jr. (1970*b*), Annual Meeting, Society of Biological Psychiatry, San Francisco, May 9.

9. Matussek, N. (1966). *Med. Mschr.*, 20:109.

10. Matussek, N. (1970). VII C.I.N.P. Congress, Prague (*in press*).

11. Matussek, N., Benkert, O., Schneider, K., Otten, H., and Pohlmeier, H. (1970). *Arzneim. Forschg. (Drug. Res.)*, 20:934.

12. Matussek, N., Pohlmeier, H., and Rüther, E. (1966). *Kl. Wschr.*, 44:727.

13. Schildkraut, J. J. (1965). *Amer. J. Psychiat.*, 122:509.

14. Vogel, W. H., Orfei, V., and Century, B. (1969). *J. Pharmac. Exp. Ther.* 165:196.

Some Current Psychobiological Studies of the Effects of L-DOPA in Depressive and Manic-Depressive Patients

William E. Bunney, Jr., Frederick K. Goodwin,
and Dennis L. Murphy

This paper reviews a group of pharmacological and behavioral studies conducted during the last several years at the National Institute of Mental Health utilizing L-3,4-dihydroxyphenylalanine (L-DOPA), the amino acid precursor of dopamine and norepinephrine, in the treatment of depressed and manic-depressed patients. The theoretical basis for these studies is the catecholamine hypothesis of affective illness, which suggests that the brain neurotransmitters, norepinephrine and/or dopamine, are functionally decreased in depression[5,17] and increased in mania.[17] The tricyclic compounds and monoamine oxidase inhibitors commonly used to treat depression increase functional levels of neurotransmitters in the brains of experimental animals and may act similarly in man.[9] It has therefore been hypothesized that this increase is related to their mode of action on behavior. However, these drugs are nonspecific in the sense that they increase functional indoleamines as well as catecholamines. Since L-DOPA has been shown to pass the blood-brain barrier and to increase brain levels and turnover of catecholamines in animals,[3,4,8,11] we administered L-DOPA in large oral doses in an attempt to evaluate more directly the postulated relationships between catecholamines and behavior.

METHODOLOGY

Figure 1 illustrates the double-blind methodology utilized in this study. L-DOPA was given on a double-blind basis to 23 patients with placebo substitution before and after the active compound. There were 10 placebo code numbers and 10 active code numbers, and the medication orders were rewritten every few days so that a patient could be changed from one placebo number to another placebo number without altering the medication. The behavior of the patients was rated every 8 hr on a scale designed to measure depressive

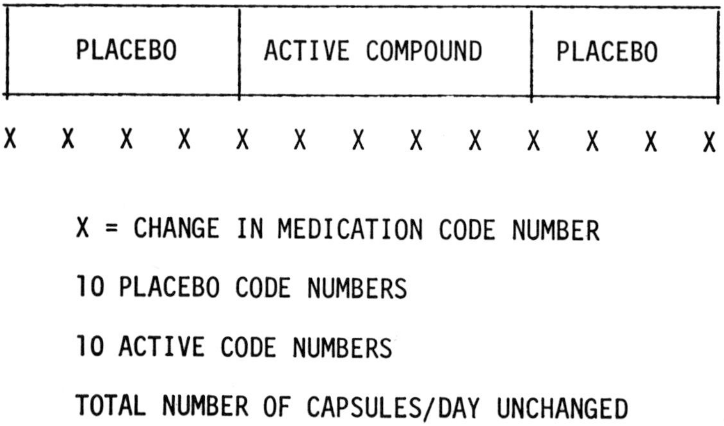

PLACEBO	ACTIVE COMPOUND	PLACEBO

X   X   X   X   X   X   X   X   X   X   X   X   X

X = CHANGE IN MEDICATION CODE NUMBER

10 PLACEBO CODE NUMBERS

10 ACTIVE CODE NUMBERS

TOTAL NUMBER OF CAPSULES/DAY UNCHANGED

FIG. 1.   Schematic diagram of double-blind methodology.

and manic behavior.[6] The nurses also completed descriptions of the patients' verbal and non-verbal behavior every 8 hr.

Figure 2 reviews the metabolism of L-DOPA. After it passes the blood-brain barrier, L-DOPA is decarboxylated to form dopamine as an intermediate compound prior to the formation of norepinephrine. As illustrated in Fig. 2, the administration of α-methyl-DOPA-hydrazine (MK485) blocks the decarboxylation of DOPA in the periphery only, since this drug does not cross the blood-brain barrier. L-DOPA was administered with and without this peripheral decarboxylase inhibitor; the average maximum dose of L-DOPA was 7 g, and the average duration of administration was 30 days. MK485 was given in daily doses of 750 to 1,000 mg; the daily dose of L-DOPA was 300 to 1,500 mg

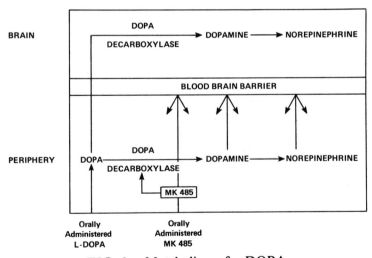

FIG. 2. Metabolism of L-DOPA.

when given in conjunction with MK485. The average duration of treatment with this combination was 30 days. MK485 has been shown to potentiate the behavioral and biochemical effects of L-DOPA in animals and in man.

In those patients who showed improvement, an immediate relapse associated with placebo substitution was noted in many cases. When observed, this rebound effect increases the level of confidence in the efficacy of a drug in an individual patient. The use of placebo substitution is important in the evaluation of drug effects because of the frequency of spontaneous remissions and exacerbations in manic-depressive illness.

Twenty-four-hour urine samples were collected throughout hospitalization for the determination of urinary catecholamines and indoleamines and their metabolites. Cerebrospinal fluid was obtained from some patients and was also analyzed for catecholamine and indoleamine metabolites. All patients studied were maintained on constant low catecholamine and indoleamine diets.

Some patients were also given high doses of probenecid as a research procedure. Probenecid inhibits the active transport of the brain biogenic amino acid metabolites, 5-hydroxyindoleacetic acid (5HIAA) and homovanillic acid (HVA), the major breakdown products of serotonin and dopamine, respectively. The cerebrospinal fluid levels of these acid metabolites are probably related to brain levels, and their rate of accumulation during probenecid administration can be used as an index of amine turnover.[13,15] The probenecid was given over the course of 12 to 18 hr in divided doses totaling 90 to 120 mg/kg to each patient, with lumbar punctures before and after the medication. Details of the procedure are presented elsewhere.[12,18]

RESULTS

Table 1 presents the overall results utilizing L-DOPA or L-DOPA plus MK485 in depressed patients. Only five out of 23 patients (25%) from the total group showed consistent improvement in depression during treatment with L-DOPA. Two of the responders received

TABLE 1. *Individual patient data*

Patient	Age	Sex	Weight (lb)	Diagnosis	Max. dose (DOPA) (g)	(mg/kg)	Response
L. R.	43	M	185	Bipolar	12.5	148	
M. M.	48	F	185	Bipolar	11.0	133	
					(1.6^a)	(19^a)	
A. C.	55	F	145	Bipolar	7.0	106	
J. L.	42	M	180	Bipolar	6.0	73	
R. M.	42	F	175	Bipolar	5.0	84	
T. J.	47	M	185	Bipolar	4.0	47	
R. J.	36	M	209	Bipolar	1.3^a	14^a	
B. H.	40	F	151	Bipolar	1.0^a	16^a	
B. C.	32	F	101	Bipolar	0.6^a	13^a	
H. R.	54	F	145	Bipolar	0.4^a	6^a	
G. A.	73	M	125	Unipolar	8.1	142	+
H. I.	60	F	138	Unipolar	8.0	128	
W. E.	55	M	158	Unipolar	8.0	112	
C. J.	47	F	150	Unipolar	8.0	100	
W. L.	52	F	140	Unipolar	7.0	110	++
					(0.3^a)	(4.7^a)	
Q. M.	24	F	140	Unipolar	7.0	110	
K. S.	46	F	160	Unipolar	4.0	55	
					(0.3^a)	(4.6^a)	
T. E.	57	F	100	Unipolar	3.0	66	
W. T.	29	M	175	Unipolar	1.5	19	
W. M.	38	F	145	Unipolar	1.4^a	21^a	+
D. D.	66	M	145	Unipolar	0.8^a	12^a	
L. F.	62	M	160	Unipolar	0.8^a	11^a	++
K. F.	44	M	165	Unipolar	0.5^a	7^a	++

^{a}MK485 plus L-DOPA.

L-DOPA alone and three received L-DOPA plus MK485. Four of these patients had relapses following placebo substitution, and three subsequently improved again on L-DOPA to the point where they were well enough to be discharged. All of the clinical responses to L-DOPA occurred among the retarded patients, and, similarly, all of the responders were in the unipolar depressed patient group (those patients without a history of mania).

The data on the patient (W. L.) with the most clear-cut behavioral response to L-DOPA are illustrated in Fig. 3. A daily L-DOPA dose of 3 g was utilized as a cut-off point in the analysis of the behavioral data in this patient because this is the minimum dose usually required to achieve a therapeutic response in parkinsonian patients. On days 1 to 33, the patient was de-

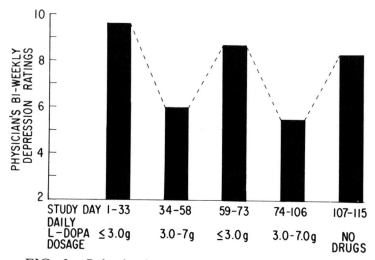

FIG. 3. Behavioral response of one patient to high doses of L-DOPA.

pressed with retarded speech and movement and appeared to have frozen facies. During the time of L-DOPA treatment in doses of 3 to 7 g per day (days 34 to 58), the first change observed was an increase in psychomotor activation. The patient was able to cry and appeared less frozen and depressed. She subsequently progressed to the point where she said she felt well and had plans for the future for the first time since admission. Following this, placebo was substituted for L-DOPA, and the patient again became sad, depressed, and retarded. She then responded again to L-DOPA (days 74 to 106) and again relapsed when placebo was substituted. Following this, she was maintained on L-DOPA after another decrease in depression and was able to leave the hospital. It should be emphasized, however, that the majority of depressed patients clearly did not respond to L-DOPA, and that in this respect this patient was unlike most other patients.

Figure 4 shows six non-responding patients who showed an intensification of existing psychotic symptoms with L-DOPA. These patients had shown a 5-day pre-drug mean psychosis rating of over 3; in each of these patients, there was an increase in psychosis during the 5 days of maximum dose. In contrast, patients without elevated psychosis ratings prior to L-DOPA showed no change in psychosis ratings during treatment.

Table 2 shows the occurrence of hypomania on L-DOPA and on L-DOPA plus MK485. Eight patients who experienced hypomanic episodes were bipolar (had histories of episodes of both mania and depression), whereas all but one of the 13 patients who showed no hypomanic episodes had unipolar depressions, thus suggesting a possible sensitivity to L-DOPA in those pa-

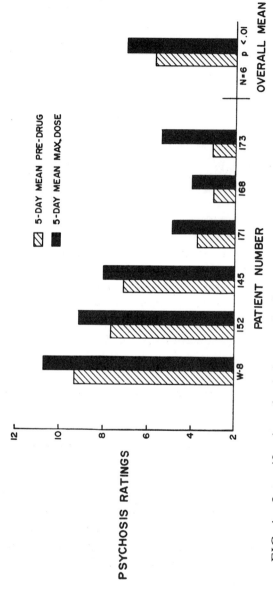

FIG. 4. Intensification of existing psychotic symptoms with L-DOPA in non-responders.

TABLE 2. *Comparison of patient and* L-DOPA *dosage characteristics in relation to the occurrence of hypomania in 22 depressed patients*

	Hypomanic episode (N = 9)	No hypomanic episode (N = 13)
Manic-depressive (bipolar) patients	8	1
Psychotic depressive (unipolar) patients	1	12
L-DOPA maximum dose (mg/kg)	99 ± 17[a] (16 ± 3)	103 ± 18 (14 ± 2)
L-DOPA treatment duration (days)	27 ± 8	29 ± 6
Age (yr)	44 ± 4	49 ± 5
Sex	4M, 5F	6M, 7F

[a] Mean ± S.E.M. The seven patients given the decarboxylase inhibitor MK485 received the L-DOPA dosage indicated in parentheses.

tients who had past histories of mania. Figure 5 shows one bipolar patient who received L-DOPA and then experienced a 2-day period during which she was talking and moving rapidly and expressing grandiose ideas. Two similar brief hypomanic episodes occurred in the patient shown in Fig. 6. These episodes were self-limited in spite of continuation of L-DOPA medication. The duration of L-DOPA treatment periods in the unipolar and bipolar patients were essentially equal. Furthermore, no episodes of hypomania developed during

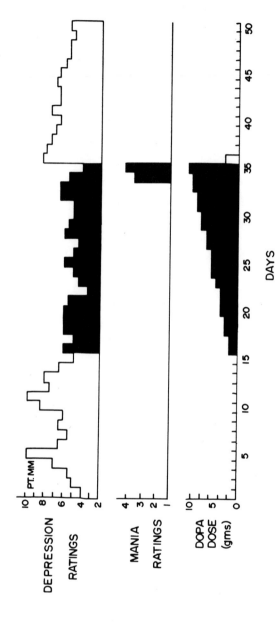

FIG. 5. Hypomania in one patient on L-DOPA.

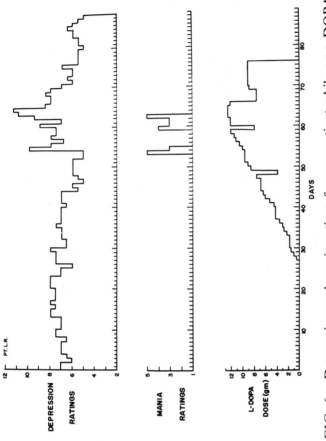

FIG. 6. Depression and mania ratings for one patient while on ʟ-DOPA.

treatment with less than 3 g of L-DOPA per day whereas all nine of the episodes developed on doses of over 3 g/day, suggesting that the hypomanic behavior represented a direct effect of the drug and not spontaneous cycles in mood.

Thus, it appears from our data that L-DOPA is clearly not an effective drug in terms of a decrease in depressive mood in the majority of patients treated. It does seem to have activating effects since it apparently increased motor and verbal activity in retarded patients and increased existing psychotic symptoms in psychotic individuals.

METABOLISM OF L-DOPA

L-DOPA has a variety of effects on brain metabolism. It increases dopamine concentrations in animal brain, and a similar change is thought to be reflected by an increase in HVA in the cerebrospinal fluid of man. In neurological patients studied at the NIMH by Dr. Thomas Chase, there was approximately a 20-fold increase in cerebrospinal fluid HVA content, and a similar increase was seen in two depressed patients who were studied simultaneously. A similar increase was noted in five patients receiving L-DOPA plus MK485. Recent work by Goodwin et al.,[12] suggests that the turnover of dopamine in brain may be increased and the turnover of serotonin decreased after large doses of L-DOPA. Comparison of changes in cerebrospinal fluid HVA and 5HIAA produced by probenecid in five patients revealed an increase in HVA accumulation and a decrease in 5HIAA during treatment with L-DOPA plus MK485. The difference between the probenecid-induced changes on and off L-DOPA was statistically significant for HVA ($p < 0.01$) and 5HIAA ($p < 0.05$). Everett and Borcherding,[9] Butcher and Engel,[7] and others have suggested that there is little or no change in brain norepinephrine in mice and rats after large doses of L-DOPA. However, Chalmers et al.[8] showed a transitory increase in norepinephrine levels and an increase in norepinephrine turnover in rat brain after 60 min following the administration of large doses of L-DOPA. Gershon et al.[11] also studied the effects of L-DOPA on norepinephrine turnover in rat brain and demonstrated that the rate of disappearance of ^{3}H-norepinephrine after cisternal injection was significantly faster in a group of L-DOPA-treated rats than in a control group, whereas the brain levels of norepinephrine were not significantly different in the two groups. This is compatible with the suggestion that L-DOPA increases synthesis and release of norepinephrine in brain.

In attempting to evaluate the metabolic actions of L-DOPA, it is important, however, to remember that, in addition to its direct effect on catecholamine levels and turnover, L-DOPA in large doses has a variety of other biochemical effects, including competition for uptake,[2] decarboxylation,[20] and storage[16] of other amine precursors and amines. L-DOPA can alter the storage of serotonin in brain and may decrease levels of this amine.[9] The administration of this amino acid in large doses is associated with a decrease in available S-adenosylmethionine and thus may interfere with other metabolic reactions involving transmethylation.[19] It has recently been suggested that L-DOPA may interfere with the function of other neurotransmitter systems, including acetylcholine and gamma-aminobutyric acid.[1]

DISCUSSION

The data that we have presented, along with those of Kanzler and Malitz and of Matussek in this volume, would suggest that L-DOPA is not effective in relieving depression, and, therefore, that a deficit in dopamine probably does not exist in most depressed patients. The occurrence of hypomania during L-DOPA treatment suggests that dopamine may be involved in this state. It is possible that hypomania and mania are different biological entities rather than being part of a continuum.

There is a remarkable consensus of opinion that DOPA is not effective in relieving depression but that it does produce an activation in man. There is also agreement that L-DOPA increases dopamine levels and dopamine turnover in man. It is not altogether clear at this point what the effects of L-DOPA are on norepinephrine metabolism in man. It may be particularly important in evaluating the effects of L-DOPA to consider these in terms of time, since its actions at 1 hr, 1 day, 1 month, or 1 year may be quite different.

REFERENCES

1. Barbeau, A., and McDowell, F. H. (Eds.): L-*DOPA and Parkinsonism.* Philadelphia, F. A. Davis, 1970.

2. Bartholini, G., Blum, J. E., and Pletscher, A.: DOPA-induced locomotor stimulation after inhibition of extracerebral decarboxylase. *J. Pharm. Pharmacol.,* 21:297–301, 1968.

3. Bertler, A., Falck, B., Ohman, C. H., and Rosengrenn, E.: The localization of monoaminergic blood-brain barrier mechanisms. *Pharmacol. Rev.,* 18:369–385, 1966.

4. Bloom, F. E., and Giarman, M. J.: Physiologic and pharmacologic considerations of biogenic amines in the nervous system. *Ann. Rev. Pharmacol.,* 8:229–258, 1968.

5. Bunney, W. E., Jr., and Davis, J. M.: Norepinephrine in depressive reactions. *Arch. Gen. Psychiat.,* 13:483, 1965.

6. Bunney, W. E., Jr., and Hamburg, D. A.: Methods for reliable longitudinal observation of behavior. *Arch. Gen. Psychiat.,* 9:280–294, 1963.

7. Butcher, L. L., and Engel, J.: Behavioral and biochemical effects of L-DOPA after peripheral decarboxylase inhibition. *Brain Res.,* 15:233–242, 1969.

8. Chalmers, J. P., Baldessarini, R. J., and Wurtman, R. J.: Effects of L-DOPA on brain norepinephrine metabolism. *Proc. Nat. Acad. Sci.,* 68:662–666, 1971.

9. Everett, G. M., and Borcherding, J. W.: L-DOPA: Effect on concentrations of dopamine, norepinephrine and serotonin in brains of mice. *Science,* 168:849–850, 1970.

10. Everett, G. M., and Wiegand, R. G.: Central amines and behavioral states: A critique and new data. *Proc. 1st Internat. Pharmacol. Mtg.,* 8:85–92, 1962.

11. Gershon, E. S., Goodwin, F. K., and Gold, P.: Effect of L-tyrosine and L-DOPA on norepinephrine (NE) turnover in rat brain *in vivo. Pharmacologist,* 12:268, 1970.

12. Goodwin, F. K., Dunner, D. L., and Gershon, E. S.: Effect of L-DOPA treatment on brain serotonin metabolism in depressed patients. *Life Sci.,* 10:751–759, 1971.

13. Neff, N. H., Tozer, T. N., and Brodie, B. B.: Application of steady-state kinetics to studies of the transfer of 5-hydroxyindoleacetic acid from brain to plasma. *J. Pharmacol. Exp. Ther.*, 158:214–218, 1967.

14. Ng, L. K. Y., Chase, T. N., Colburn, R. W., and Kopin, I. J.: L-DOPA-induced release of cerebral monoamines. *Science*, 170:76, 1970.

15. Roos, B. E., and Sjostrom, R.: 5-Hydroxyindoleacetic acid (and homovanillic acid) levels in the cerebrospinal fluid after probenecid application in patients with manic-depressive psychosis. *Pharmacol. Clin.*, 1:153–155, 1969.

16. Scheckel, C. L., Boff, E., and Pazery, L. M.: Hyperactive states related to the metabolism of norepinephrine and similar biochemicals. *Ann. N.Y. Acad. Sci.*, 159:939, 1969.

17. Schildkraut, J. J.: The catecholamine hypothesis of affective disorders: A review of supporting evidence. *Amer. J. Psychiat.*, 122:509, 1965.

18. Tamarkin, N. R., Goodwin, F. K., and Axelrod, J.: Rapid elevations of homovanillic acid (HVA) and 5-hydroxyindoleacetic acid (5HIAA) in human cerebrospinal fluid following probenecid administration. *Pharmacologist*, 12:198, 1970.

19. Wurtman, R. J., Rose, C. M., Matthysse, S., Stephenson, J., and Baldessarini, R.: L-Dihydroxyphenylalanine: Effect on S-adenosylmethionine in brain. *Science*, 169:395, 1970.

20. Yuwiler, A., Geller, E., and Eiduson, S.: Studies on 5-hydroxytryptophan decarboxylase. I. *In vitro* inhibition and substrate interaction. *Arch. Biochem. Biophys.*, 80:162–173, 1959.

L-DOPA for the Treatment of Depression

Maureen Kanzler and Sidney Malitz

In the course of L-DOPA therapy for Parkinson's disease, some investigators noted that an alleviation of depression occurred in many patients. They wondered if this anti-depressant effect were due primarily to the drug or if it were secondary to the patient's awareness of improvement in his parkinson symptoms, resulting in increased mobility and consequent renewal of interest in life around him. To assess the efficacy of L-DOPA as an anti-depressant, we decided to administer L-DOPA to patients whose primary diagnosis was one of depression.

SUBJECTS

Nine patients were treated with L-DOPA in the Department of Experimental Psychiatry at New York State Psychiatric Institute from February 1969 through June 1970. Of these patients, five were female and four were male. The female patients ranged in age from 57 to 64, with a mean age of 60 years. The male patients were more disparate in age, ranging from 33 to 67 years with a mean age of 52 years.

All patients had been admitted to the hospital because of severe depression. Target symptoms which warranted the patient's inclusion in the study were: insomnia, anorexia, weight loss, inability to function in daily routine, feelings of worthlessness, hopelessness, suicidal ideation or attempt. Not all these symptoms had to be present in each patient, but those which were present were sufficient in quantity or quality to warrant hospitalization.

Diagnostically, three patients were classified as suffering from neurotic depressive reaction, and six from psychotic depressive reaction. Although the protocol stipulated that subjects were to be non-parkinsonian, we *did* have in our study two parkinsonian patients — one who was recognized as having parkinsonism after he was started in the study and one who showed the residue of a drug-induced parkinsonism. In both cases, however, the presenting problem was one of severe depression which had antedated any signs of parkinsonism.

Six of our patients had long psychiatric histories, having suffered recurrent depressions over many years. However, only three of these had been hospitalized before the current admission. For the other three patients, the present illness was of an acute nature, necessitating their first psychiatric treatment and hospitalization. None of the nine gave a history of manic episodes.

Viewing these subjects in regard to placement on an agitation–retardation continuum, four would fall toward the agitated extreme. Two seemed more retarded, and three showed a mixture of psychomotor inhibition and elements of restlessness and tension.

DOSAGE REGIMEN

Our dosage plan evolved with our first patient. It had been planned to begin with 750 mg per day and increase the dose by 500 mg per day on alternate days until a favorable clinical response occurred or until side effects required cutting back. The maximum dose anticipated was 8,000 mg/day. During the treatment of the first patient, however, it was found that staff limitations over weekends made it more feasible to increase dosage by 250 mg daily on Monday through Thursday, with a stabilization at the Thursday level for the weekend.

Active medication, as well as placebo, was packaged in two sizes of capsule — 250 and 500 mg. Patients received the same number of capsules every day throughout the length of the study. At the beginning of the study, all the capsules a patient received contained placebo. Dosage increments were made by substituting active for placebo capsules, so that the patient never knew that he was getting anything different one day to the next. The total daily dosage was divided into three administrations — 8 A.M., noon, and 5 P.M. If severe side effects made it necessary to stop increasing the amount of active substance, the dosage level would be held constant until the side effect disappeared, or, if necessary for patient welfare, the dosage was reduced.

Insofar as maximum dosages are concerned, only one patient achieved the permitted maximum of 8,000 mg per day. This was the patient who was found to be suffering from parkinsonism. Three patients reached 3,000 mg; three reached 4,000 mg; and two reached 4,500 mg.

All patients had an initial placebo trial for at least

a week. This trial was followed by active medication. There was a final placebo week for six patients. The range of time on active medication was four to six weeks for the non-parkinsonian patients. The two patients with parkinsonian signs tolerated much longer treatment — nine weeks for one and seventeen for the other, the latter being discharged while still receiving a maintenance dose of L-DOPA.

LABORATORY TESTS

Laboratory tests, including CBC, hematocrit, SGOT, SGPT, BUN, alkaline phosphatase, and urinalysis were performed at baseline and at intervals throughout the study. No remarkable changes occurred in these measures.

EVALUATION PROCEDURES

As is customary with all our in-patient studies, patients were interviewed and evaluated at weekly conferences. Senior members of the psychiatric team (psychiatrists, research psychologist, head nurse) used a number of rating scales in assessing the condition of each patient. One set of global ratings covered Degree of Mental Illness, Anxiety, Depression, and Change. In addition, the Brief Psychiatric Rating Scale (BPRS) of Overall and Gorham[5] was completed. At these conferences, ward personnel (nurses, social workers, occupational therapist, and students) reported on the patient's behavior during the preceding week. Plans for the next week's treatment were discussed, including whatever alterations of dosage might be necessary because of side effects.

RESULTS

Pre- and post-treatment mean ratings for the group of nine patients are shown in the accompanying Table 1, "Pretreatment vs Post-treatment Mean Scores of Nine Patients Receiving L-DOPA for Depression." Each rating was made on a seven-point scale, on which a rating of "1" meant "not sick at all." At the other end of the continuum, a "7" indicated "extremely severe"

TABLE 1. *Pretreatment vs. Post-treatment mean scores of nine patients receiving L-DOPA for depression*

	Pretreatment mean score	Post-treatment mean score	Difference	t
Clinical rating scale				
degree of mental illness	5.2	4.1	1.1	3.50[a]
anxiety	4.5	3.6	0.9	2.77[b]
depression	5.2	3.8	1.4	3.12[b]
change		2.9		
Brief psychiatric rating scale				
somatic concern	3.6	2.7	0.9	2.72[b]
anxiety	5.1	4.1	1.0	2.46[b]
emotional withdrawal	1.7	1.3	0.4	1.92
concept disorganization	1.3	1.1	0.2	1.00
guilt	1.9	1.5	0.4	1.22
tension	3.4	2.7	0.7	1.45
mannerisms	1.5	1.1	0.4	1.20
grandiosity	1.0	1.1	−0.1	0.99
depressive mood	5.1	3.6	1.5	3.08[b]
hostility	2.5	1.7	0.8	2.75
suspiciousness	1.9	1.3	0.6	1.45
hallucinations	1.1	1.0	0.1	1.00
motor retardation	3.5	2.2	1.3	4.45[a]
uncooperativeness	1.5	1.7	−0.2	0.46
unusual thought	1.7	1.3	0.4	0.83
blunted affect	1.9	1.7	0.2	0.55

[a] Significant at 0.01 level.
[b] Significant at 0.05 level.

illness in the area being rated. The "change" score reflected amount of change since the beginning of the study and went from "1 — very much improved" through "4 — no change" to "7 — very much worse."

The first column of the table gives the pretreatment mean scores of our group, that is, the average of the staff ratings on each of the scales, rated at the end of the initial placebo period. The preplacebo rating was not used, although the data are available. It was thought that the use of the postplacebo rating as a baseline would give a more meaningful comparison with the post-treatment score by eliminating some of the so-called "placebo effect" of receiving a pill. The post-treatment score is the average staff rating at the time of discontinuation of active medication.

The first column of the table indicates that the group as a whole was considered slightly more than "markedly ill" on the global scales assessing Degree of Mental Illness and Depression, and on the BPRS scales of Anxiety and Depressive Mood. There was a somewhat lower rating on the global scale of Anxiety, reflecting a difference in instructions given to raters on the two scales in regard to this symptom. On the global scale, raters were left free to assess the patient's anxiety in the light of their total clinical experience, whereas on the BPRS Anxiety scale, they were constrained to assess "worry, fear, or over-concern for present or future" and to "rate solely on the basis of verbal report of patient's own subjective experiences." Three other scales of the BPRS showed at least "mild" illness — Somatic Concern, Tension, and Motor Retardation. The scales which generally reflect a more florid psychopathology show rather low ratings, so that we can say, as a whole, that the members of the subject group were not withdrawn emotionally; their thinking processes were generally organized and logical, even if slowed down; there was a little paranoid ideation and no grandiosity and only a small amount of expressed hostility or uncooperativeness. Expression of affect might be dulled or limited by the depression, but no patient showed a schizophrenic-like blunting of affect.

After treatment, there was a small but statistically significant improvement on the three global scales and on the BPRS subscales measuring Somatic Concern, Anxiety, Depressive Mood, and Motor Retardation. (The statistical significance of the mean differences pre- vs. post treatment were assessed by a *t* test for correlated means.) Insofar as the "Change" score was concerned, the mean rating reflects "minimally improved." The individual ratings of Change were distributed as follows:

Very much improved — one patient
Much improved — two patients
Minimally improved — three patients
Unchanged — two patients
Minimally worse — one patient

How much of the improvement reflected by the difference in mean ratings was due to L-DOPA treatment is open to question. We have often seen patients who were admitted to the hospital as seriously depressed improve markedly without medication. The hospitalization renders them secure from the outside stresses temporarily at least, and within the hospital's protective environment many target symptoms may be alleviated.

Also, it is possible that improvement occurs in

depressed patients simply by being given a pill or capsule by a concerned therapist. For example, in an outpatient study reported at the San Francisco meeting of the American Psychiatric Association last May in which the same assessment measures were used, the placebo group pre- vs. post-treatment differences on the global scales were as follows:

Scale	Pre- vs. post-treatment difference scores
Degree of mental illness	1.1
Anxiety	0.8
Depression	1.8

The Change score rating was 2.4. It was found in that study that, with an average N of 25 in each of eight groups, an active treatment had to show a difference of more than two points to be statistically superior to placebo. We feel this requirement of a two-point difference on pre- vs. post-treatment ratings is clinically valid, apart from any evaluation of *statistical* significance.

Measured against this more demanding clinical criterion of improvement, the scales relevant for our L-DOPA patients showed the following. On the global scales of Degree of Mental Illness, two patients showed sufficient improvement, on the Anxiety scale one patient, and on the Depression scale three patients. On the BPRS subscales, one patient showed satisfactory improvement in Somatic Concern, two on the Anxiety scale, one on the Motor Retardation scale, and four on the Depressive Mood Scale. On the Tension scale, one patient exceeded the two-point requirement in the positive direction but one also in the negative direction.

Generally speaking, these results do not indicate

that L-DOPA is an effective anti-depressant for the usual depressed patient. However, some *did* improve and their improvement poses questions.

SIDE EFFECTS

We have reported elsewhere in detail concerning the side effects experienced by our patients during the L-DOPA treatment. Side effects differed greatly from patient to patient and included varying degrees and frequency of nausea, vomiting, jitteriness, dizziness, insomnia, tension, confusion, panic, and rage. Presence of side effects did not appear to have any clear relationship to change in depression.

EXPLANATION OF FIGURES

Three graphs have been prepared to illustrate the relationship between dosage level and change in depression ratings (Figs. 1-3). The first charts the course of a patient whose depression disappeared during her treatment. The second plots the progress of a patient who became worse and shifted from agitated to retarded depression. The third outlines the course of a depressed patient with parkinsonism.

Patient No. 5, whose graph appears in Fig. 1, was a 57-year-old female, admitted to the hospital for her fourth episode of psychotic depression. Prior episodes has been treated primarily with ECT. Presenting symptoms included depressed mood, inability to work on her job or at home, prolonged periods of staring straight ahead, crying episodes, and self-referential ideation with suspicions that she was being laughed at or mocked.

There was no improvement during the placebo

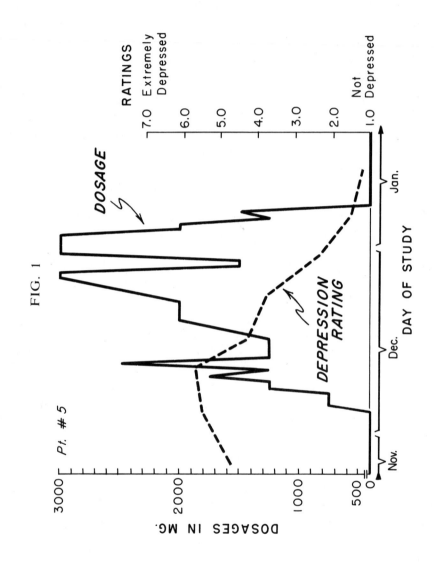

FIG. 1

Pt. # 5

RATINGS

7.0 Extremely
    Depressed

6.0

5.0

4.0

3.0

2.0

1.0 Not
    Depressed

DOSAGE

DEPRESSION
RATING

Nov.   Dec.   Jan.

DAY OF STUDY

3000

2000

1000

500

0

DOSAGES IN MG.

week. The patient began treatment with 750 mg a day and developed nausea on the second day of treatment. She continued to experience nausea throughout the entire course. On the seventh day, she had nausea and vomiting, appeared very confused in thinking, and was disoriented for time. This confusion persisted for several days after medication was reduced. Despite the severity of side effects, the patient's depression began to improve during this time of possible toxic delirium and continued to improve despite the nausea and vomiting which persisted throughout her time on active medication.

Figure 2 illustrates the course of the seventh patient studied, a 64-year-old female admitted after approximately nine months of depression. Target symptoms were sadness, agitation, insomnia, anorexia, weight loss, and difficulty in concentration associated with obsessive ruminations. This patient had had two episodes of depression in her earlier adulthood, but had functioned adequately for 20 years before the present illness. In the early stages of this episode, the patient had been treated briefly by three therapists with antidepressants and tranquilizers. Exactly which drugs were used was not known, although the patient recalled having experienced some improvement while on medication.

This patient also did not improve during the placebo week. Unlike the patient discussed above who developed nausea on the second day of treatment, this patient tolerated the course of medication until the eighth day, when she complained of nausea, vomiting, agitation, and sweating. Despite side effects, her medication increases proceeded to a maximum of 4,000 mg/day, when the side

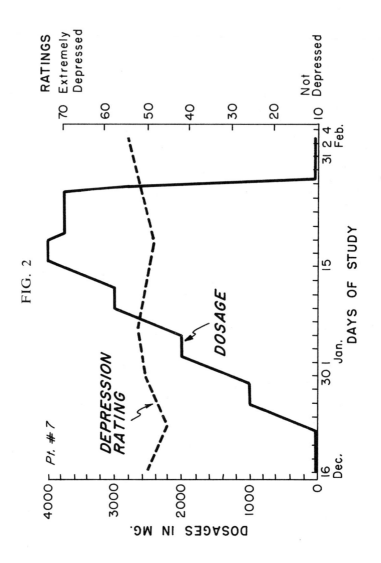

FIG. 2

effects (nausea, vomiting, headache) became so severe that dosage was reduced. Despite this reduction, she experienced time disorientation and, some days later, further G.I. distress, urinary retention, constipation, and palpitations. Emotionally this patient became more withdrawn as the top dosage was attained and then reduced. On the final placebo week, the G.I. distress abated but jitteriness continued. After the study was terminated, the patient was started on imipramine (25 mg t.i.d.) but she became more agitated. She was then given amitriptyline (25 mg t.i.d.) but her condition continued to deteriorate. She became increasingly agitated, screaming, disrobing, and lying on the floor. At times she appeared totally out of contact with reality. She did not improve until she received a course of electroshock therapy. After ECT, she maintained her improvement on amitriptyline (50 mg t.i.d.) and chlorpromazine (100 mg h.s.). There is a puzzling inconsistency, therefore, in this patient's reaction to amitriptyline on the two trials, with L-DOPA preceding one administration and not the other.

In contrast to the above two patients, the patient whose course of treatment is graphed in Fig. 3, showed a comparatively uneventful, slow but even progress. This subject was a 67-year-old male diagnosed as suffering from a retarded psychotic depression with anorexia, weight loss, insomnia, psychomotor retardation, and somatic delusions. This was his fourth admission in less than four years. On the first three admissions, he had been treated with electroshock therapy with good but transient results. In view of the short-lived nature of his improvement with ECT, it was decided that a course of high-level doses of imipramine should be tried. He

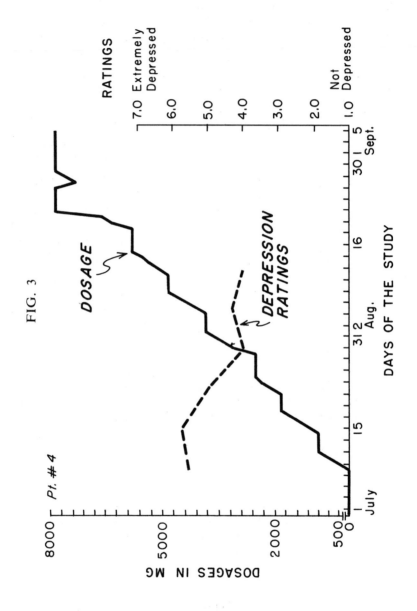

FIG. 3

proved unable to tolerate more than 75 mg t.i.d., at which level he showed marked and persistent postural hypotension without improvement in his depression.

As indicated in Fig. 3, the upward step-wise progression of increase in dosage of L-DOPA proceeded evenly to the 8,000 mg/day level. There was some dizziness at the first increase after 4,000 mg, which was associated with a paradoxical increase in lying to sitting blood pressure. No further discomfort was reported until the 8,000 mg/day level, when he complained of nausea for the first time and again of dizziness.

Staff ratings for this patient were done through five weeks and show a gradual improvement in his depression. This improvement continued after the rating period was over and while his dosage increased to the maximum. He remained at this maximum level to discharge.

DISCUSSION

Bunney and his associates have reported[1-4] improvement of depression in some of their patients who received L-DOPA, alone or in combination with MK485. In their investigations, the positive response was confined to patients who suffered from retarded depression and to only some of these.

With our subjects, we did not find this exclusive association of positive response with pretreatment retardation. In fact, we cannot link type of response consistently with any variable.

Further, Bunney's group in a recent article[4] observed that most of their non-responders subsequently responded to tricyclic anti-depressants. With our patients, a good response to a tricyclic might or might not occur. For example, one patient who made only slight gains on L-DOPA showed a sudden improvement on the tenth day of imipramine (100 mg/day). Two with minimal gains on L-DOPA showed only slight improvement on subsequent nortriptyline. The rapid decompensation of a patient who did poorly on tricyclics after L-DOPA has been discussed in relation to the second graph (Fig. 2).

It would appear that the clinical picture labelled "depression" is the final common behavior resulting from various biochemical imbalances. These, in turn, probably are determined, at least in part, by the pharmacogenetic make-up of the patient.

That patients differ in response to drugs is manifest. In our laboratory, we have begun to tease out these differences—although not, as yet, in regard to L-DOPA. We are studying variations of blood levels of imipramine in relation to changes in dosage and both of these variables in relation to clinical response.

The present difficulty in the classification of depressions may result from the inclusion under the one heading of many different subtypes. We have gone as far as we can in the descriptive approach to the nosology of depression. Perhaps we need to look now to biochemical techniques to aid us—not only in diagnosis but also in specific treatment. And in this exploration of the biochemistry of depression, we may learn more from the intensive study of the atypical patient whose blood levels do not follow the usual pattern of the majority of patients, whatever the reason may be—pharmacogenetic or otherwise.

REFERENCES

1. Bunney, W. E., Janowsky, D. S., Goodwin, F. K., Davis, J. M., Brodie, H. K., Murphy, D. L., and Chase, T. N. (1969): Effect of L-DOPA in depression. *Lancet,* 1:885–886.

2. Bunney, W. E., Murphy, D. L., Brodie, H. K., and Goodwin, F. K. (1970): L-DOPA in depressed patients. *Lancet,* 1:352.

3. Goodwin, F. K., Brodie, H. K., and Murphy, D. L. L-DOPA catecholamines and behavior. A clinical and biochemical study in depressed patients *(unpublished).*

4. Goodwin, F. K., Brodie, H. K., Murphy, D. L., and Bunney, W. E. (1970): Administration of a peripheral decarboxylase inhibitor with L-DOPA to depressed patients. *Lancet,* 1:908–911.

5. Overall, J. E., and Gorham, D. R. (1962): The brief Psychiatric Rating Scale. *Psychological Reports,* 10:799–812.

L-DOPA: A Psychiatric Tool

Jose Yaryura-Tobias, Bruce Diamond, and Sidney Merlis

The high incidence of psychiatric disorders as concomitant side effects in the use of high doses of L-DOPA in the treatment of Parkinson's disease has renewed interest in this compound as a metabolic tool in psychiatric research.

In the past, L-DOPA was used to investigate behavioral properties of catecholamine systems in animal and human brains. The administration of DOPA with or without a monoamine oxidase inhibitor (MAOI) in animals produced various psychophysiological responses, usually related to dose and species tested. Symptoms included alertness, responsiveness, irritability and aggressiveness,[1] biting behavior,[2] catatonic stupor and rage.[3] However, other investigators reported the combination of L-DOPA and MAOI depress searching activities in rats[4] and mice.[5] In the chick, L-DOPA caused akinesia.[6] In cats pretreated with phenilazine, the administration of L-DOPA caused shrieking, defensiveness, probable hallucinations, and attempts to escape.[7] Also, small doses of L-DOPA in the cat caused motoneural excitability and blocked excitatory effects of Group II and III afferent fibers, and larger doses blocked the inhibitory actions mediated by the flexor reflex afferents.[8] The action of L-DOPA on depression is covered by Matussek and Goodwin elsewhere in this volume.

According to various authors,[9-16] the evidence of psychiatric symptoms during the treatment of Parkinson's disease with L-Dopa has ranged from 2.5 to 55.5%. Behavioral manifestations have included assaultiveness, aggressiveness, increased libido, and withdrawal. Delusions, perceptual changes, confusion, lack of judgment, and impaired memory and orientation were also reported. In other patients, agitation, acute anxiety, depression, fatigue, and insomnia were observed. Jenkins and Groh[17] reported alertness, euphoria, and memory improvement.

According to Boshes,[18] no intellectual changes were observed with L-DOPA, yet Meir and Martin[19] found a significant augment in the WAIS, mainly on the perceptual organization deviation quotient.

Our own experience with parkinson patients has demonstrated aggravation of pre-existent depression, agitated depression, suicidal ideation, assaultiveness, paranoid thinking and auditory and visual hallucinations.[20] In this experiment, we observed that psychiatric symptoms became apparent at the time patients showed neurological improvement. For others, the chance of neurological improvement was affected by the presence of dementia.[14] The same trends seem to be followed by patients with associated chronic brain syndrome or Parkinson's disease consequent to encephalitis.[21]

In our experience with L-DOPA in schizophrenics

with drug-induced parkinsonism, we observed a significant mental and neurological deterioration.[22]

Finally, Celesia and Barr[16] reported an association between dyskinesia and psychiatric disturbances in 87.5% of their L-DOPA cases.

L-DOPA IN SCHIZOPHRENICS

The administration of L-DOPA to psychotic patients with or without neuroleptic medication in amounts varying between 1 and 2 g daily has caused an aggravation of their psychoses without symptoms of toxic delirium.[23] In two cases of alcoholic psychosis, an elevation of mood was observed in one and depression in the other. Some patients showed alertness, optimism, and elaboration of their future, while others noticed increased sexual urge. Verbal communication was significantly improved.

Employing this line of reasoning, we placed a 16-year-old autistic patient on L-DOPA 100 mg b.i.d. Presently, there is initial evidence indicating that he has begun to attend to his surroundings and is attempting to converse.

DISCUSSION

In order to explain the psychiatric symptoms in L-DOPA-treated parkinson patients, the following explanations are offered: (1) a pre-existent psychosis or dementia; (2) a subclinical or latent psychosis; (3) an untoward reaction; and (4) a new clinical entity (chemical psychosis).

For many years there has been a feeling that a functional relationship exists between the caudate nucleus and schizophrenia.[24]   Gross behavioral changes have been caused by lesion or stimulation in the caudate, both in animal and human experimentation.[25-30]   Histological changes in the basal ganglia were found in parkinson patients with mental symptoms, suffering from chronic manganese poisoning and carbon monoxide intoxication.   In the parkinsonian dementia of the Chamorro-speaking people of Guam, cell loss occurred in the locus coeruleus, substantia nigra, substantia innominata, and often the globus pallidus, sometimes with severe generalized brain atrophy.[31,32]   Thus, the possibility of the caudate nucleus having a higher nervous activity must be considered.

There is sufficient evidence that L-DOPA exerts a dual action in the CNS—neurological and psychiatric. Therefore, the possibility of a histochemical complex that plays an interconnecting role between some forms of mental illness and behavior may exist.

The administration of L-DOPA to psychotic patients, manifested by mental changes, would imply an aggravation of their illness, either by augmenting an etiological factor or by drug toxicity.   However, our patients indicated the exacerbation of their mental symptoms was a continuation of their primary illness, i.e., schizophrenia.

Two observations were made in schizophrenics with drug-induced parkinsonism treated with L-DOPA: (1) a worsening of their mental status in spite of high amounts of neuroleptics given; and (2) the ineffectiveness of L-DOPA to suppress the neurological symptoms. A competitive action between L-DOPA and neuroleptics can explain these findings.   Some studies have indicated that chlorpromazine depletes dopamine (DA) content in cat brain[33] and interferes with the metabolism of L-DOPA in rat brain.[34]

Also, chlorpromazine and haloperidol caused a significant increase in DA and homovanillic acid (HVA) in urinary excretions of schizophrenics with drug-induced parkinsonism.[35] On the other hand, L-DOPA antagonized reserpine-induced parkinsonism.[36] Therefore the following statements can be made.

(1) L-DOPA improves the neurological symptoms of Parkinson's disease and causes mental symptoms similar to those found in schizophrenia.

(2) The administration of L-DOPA worsens the neuropsychiatric symptoms of schizophrenic patients with drug-induced parkinsonism.

(3) L-DOPA aggravates schizophrenia.

(4) Neuroleptics, while arresting psychotic symptoms, might produce parkinsonism.

What is the relationship, if any, between schizophrenia and parkinson states and their pharmacological interaction with L-DOPA and neuroleptics?

If minimal drug-induced parkinsonism is necessary for neuroleptic efficacy and if DA is thereby depleted, the presence of psychiatric symptoms in L-DOPA-treated patients would be caused by an excess of dopamine, after the parkinson symptoms are controlled. This remnant would follow various pathways originating symptoms in different parts of the brain (delusions, increased libido, dyskinesia). The action of L-DOPA with schizophrenic patients tends to support the catecholamine theories of schizophrenia.

In addition, it is important to remember the chemical resemblance between L-DOPA and certain psychotomimetics, such as mescaline and its derivatives.

If schizophrenia is the result of a pathological trans-methylation, and if L-DOPA is abnormally metabolized, will nicotinic acid, a methyl acceptor, modify this process? For this reason, we administered nicotinic acid to L-DOPA-treated schizophrenic patients. Initial findings indicate that a variety of changes occur. It appears to us that L-DOPA, a naturally occurring substance in animal and man which causes behavioral and psychiatric modifications, offers a good opportunity to explore truthfully the biochemical aspects of psychoses with the focus based on alterations in the metabolism of the biogenic amines.

REFERENCES

1. Everett, G. M. (1961): Some electrophysiological and biochemical correlates of motor activity and aggressive behaviour. Proceedings of the Second International Meeting of the Collegium Internationale Neuro-Psychopharmacologicum, Basle, 1960. *Neuropharmacology, 2:*49–84.

2. Katz, M. H., Yen-Koo, H. C., and Krop, S. (1967): The effects of psychoactive drugs in 3,4-dihydroxyphenilalanine (D-L-DOPA) induced excitation in mice. *Fed. Proc., 26:* 289.

3. Vander Wende, C., and Spoerlein, M. T. (1962): Psychotic symptoms induced in mice by the intravenous administration of solutions of 3,4-dihydroxyphenilalanine (DOPA). *Arch. Int. Pharmacodyn., 137:*145–154.

4. Scheel-Kruger, J., and Randrup, A. (1967): Stereotype hyperactive behavior produced by dopamine in the absence of noradrenaline. *Life Sciences, 6:*1389–1398.

5. Fisher, E. (1965): Monoamine oxidase inhibitors. *Lancet,* 2:245–246.

6. Spooner, C. E., and Winters, W. D. (1964): Behavioral, EEG and blood pressure effects of centrally acting drugs in the chick. *The Pharmacologist,* 6:171.

7. Reis, D. J., Moorehead, D. T., II, and Merlino, N. (1970): Dopa-induced excitement in the cat. *Arch. Neurol.,* 22: 31–38.

8. Baker, R. G., and Anderson, E. G. (1970): The effects of L-3,4-dihydroxyphenilalanine on spinal reflex activity. *J. Pharmacol. Exptl. Therap.,* 173:212–223.

9. Calne, D. B., Spiers, A. S. D., Stern, G. M., Laurence, D. R., and Armitage, P. (1969): L-DOPA in idiopathic parkinsonism. *Lancet,* 2:973–976.

10. Barbeau, A. (1969): L-DOPA therapy in Parkinson's disease: A critical review of nine years experience. *Canad. Med. Ass. J.,* 101:791–800.

11. Cotzias, G. C., Papavasiliou, P. S., and Gellene, R. (1969): Modification of parkinsonism, chronic treatment with L-DOPA. *New England Journal of Medicine,* 280:337–345.

12. Goodwin-Austen, R. B., Tomlinson, E. B., Frears, C. C., and Kok, H. W. L. (1969): Effects of L-DOPA on Parkinson's disease. *Lancet,* 2:165–168.

13. Yahr, M. D., Duvoisin, R. C., Schear, M. J., Barrett, R. E., and Hoehn, M. M. (1969): Treatment of parkinsonism with levodopa. *Arch. Neurol.,* 21:343–354.

14. McDowell, F., Lee, J., Swift, T., Sweet, R. D., Ogsbury, J. S., and Kessler, J. T. (1969): Treatment of Parkinson's syndrome with L-dihydroxyphenilalanine (levodopa). *Annals of Int. Med.,* 72:29–35.

15. Klawans, H. L., and Garvin, J. S. (1969): Treatment of parkinsonism with L-DOPA. *Dis. Nerv. Syst.,* 30:737–746.

16. Celesia, G. G., and Barr, A. N. (1970): Psychosis and other psychiatric manifestations of levodopa therapy. *Arch. Neur.,* 23:193–200.

17. Jenkins, R. B., and Groh, R. H. (1970): Psychic effects in patients treated with levodopa. *JAMA,* 212:2265.

18. Boshes, B., Blonsky, E. R., Arbit, J. and Klein, K. (1969): Effect of L-DOPA on individual symptoms of parkinsonism. *Trans. Amer. Neurol. Assoc.,* 94:229–231.

19. Meir, M. J., and Martin, W. E. (1070): Intellectual changes associated with levodopa therapy. *JAMA,* 213:465–466.

20. Yaryura-Tobias, J. A., Diamond, B., and Merlis, S. The action of L-DOPA on behavior. Presented at the First Multistate Conference of the Eastern Psychiatric Association, April 17, 1970 in New York.

21. Sacks, O. W., Meereloff, C., Schwartz, W., Golfarb, A., and Kohn, M. (1970): Effects of L-DOPA in patients with dementia. *Lancet,* I:1231.

22. Yaryura-Tobias, J. A., Wolpert, A., Dana, L., and Merlis, S. (1970): Action of L-DOPA in drug induced extrapyramidalism. *Dis. Nerv. Syst.,* 31:60–63.

23. Yaryura-Tobias, J. A., Diamond, B., and Merlis, S. (1970): The action of L-DOPA on schizophrenic patients (A preliminary report). *Curr. Ther. Res.,* 12:528–531.

24. Mettler, F. A. (1955): Perceptual capacity, functions of the corpus striatum and schizophrenia. *Psychiat. Quart.,* 29:89–111.

25. Akert, K., and Anderson, B. (1951): Experimenteller Beitrag zur Physiologie des Nucleus Cadatus. *Acta Physiol. Scand.,* 22:281–298.

26. Heath, R. G., and Hodes, R. (1952): Induction of sleep by stimulation of the caudate nucleus in *Macaco rhesus* and man. *Trans. Amer. Neurol. Ass.,* 77:204–205.

27. Buchwald, N. A., and Ervin, F. R. (1957): Evoked potentials and behavior. A study of responses to subcortical stimulation in the awake, unrestrained animal. *Electroenceph. Clin. Neurophysiol.,* 9:477–496.

28. Formau, D., and Ward, J. W. (1957): Response to electrical stimulation of caudate nucleus in cats in chronic experiments. *J. Neurophysiol.,* 20:230–244.

29. Dean, W. H., and Davis, G. D. (1969): Behavior changes following caudate lesions in the Rhesus monkey. *J. Neurophysiol.,* 22:524–537.

30. Van Buren, N. M. (1963): Confusion and disturbance of speech from stimulation in vicinity of the head of the caudate nucleus. *J. Neurosurg.,* 20:148–157.

31. Kurland, L. T., and Mulder, D. W. (1954): Epidemiologic investigations of amyotrophic lateral esderosis. 1. Preliminary report on geographic distribution, with special ref-

erences to the Mariana Islands, including clinical and pathological observations. *Neurology,* 4:355–378, 438–448.

32. Brody, J. A., and Chen, K. M. (1968): Changing epidemiologic patterns of amyotrophic lateral sclerosis and parkinsonism-dementia on Guam. Motor-Neuron Disease. In: *Research on Amyotrophic Lateral Sclerosis and Related Disorders* Vol. 2, edited by F. H. Norris, Jr. and L. T. Kurland, 61–79. Grune and Stratton, New York.

33. Laverty, R., and Sharman, D. F. (1965): Modification by drugs of the metabolism of 3,4-dihydroxyphenylethylamine, noradrenaline and 5-hydroxytryptamine in the brain. *Brit. J. Pharmacol.,* 24:759–762.

34. Gey, K. F., and Pletscher, A. (1964): Effects of chlorpromazine on the metabolism of DL-2-C¹⁴-DOPA in the rat. *J. Pharmacol. Exptl. Therap.,* 145:337–343.

35. Bruno, A., and Allegranza, A. (1965): The effect of haloperidol on the urinary excretion of dopamine, homovanillic and vanilmandelic acids in schizophrenics. *Psychopharmacologia (Berlin),* 8:60–66.

36. Degkwitz, R., Frowein, R., Kulenkampff, G., and Mohs, V. (1960): Uber die Wirkungen des L-DOPA beim Menschen und deren Beeinflussung durch Reserpin, Chlorpromazin, Iproniazid und Vitamin B₆. *Klin. Wschr.,* 38:120–123.

Some Biochemical, Pharmacological, and Genetic Approaches to the Problem of Mood and Depression

Guy M. Everett

In 1959, Everett and Toman,[4] on the basis of their studies of the reversal of reserpine depression in mice and monkeys with DL-DOPA, first proposed the biogenic amine hypothesis of depression (inadequate amines) and mania (excess amines). In their summary, they projected their studies to man as follows:

> The fact that essentially similar reversal of deserpidine effects with desoxyephedrine or DOPA was also observed in rats and monkeys leads to speculation regarding the same mechanisms in man. One may speculate on the possible role of centrally active amines present in the brain in the normal activity and general responsiveness of an individual. An excess of these might result in irritability, restlessness and aggressiveness. In the opposite direction, a deficiency of these substances would result in depressions and general lassitude. The favorable response to iproniazid therapy would in this scheme result from the increase in central catechol amines after inhibiting monoamine oxidase, an enzyme that metabolizes these amines.

At the time, this seemed an audacious hypothesis, but in recent years various lines of evidence have supported this hypothesis,[8] and clinical studies have been conducted to explore this possibility.

The reversal of depression with L-DOPA has not been clearly substantiated. Although a few patients showed favorable changes in mood, most patients showed increased motor activity and some agitation.[1] In a study of patients with a history of hypomania, L-DOPA was quite effective in bringing about hypomanic behavior.[6] This supports the hypothesis that mania may be precipitated by excess amines. These refer to the amines available to receptors. In these early studies, both norepinephrine and dopamine were considered together, although more recent work suggests these two amines may in some instances be antagonistic rather than synergistic in their central actions.[3]

The role of serotonin in depression is under extensive study, but results remain equivocal at best.[2] The precursor of serotonin, 5-hydroxytryptophan, does not reverse reserpine depression in mice or monkeys.[4] Nevertheless, at this stage we cannot exclude a possible role of all the amines in the etiology of depression. No matter how these amines are involved in depression, they should be considered as trigger mechanisms which set off behavioral patterns of great complexity. The brain levels of amines as well as certain behavioral patterns and predispositions are undoubtedly genetically determined. Studies in strains of mice show wide differences in the brain levels of the three amines. Strains tend to have high or low levels of all three amines. The levels of dopamine, norepinephrine, and serotonin are highly constant in a given strain. The ability of a strain to synthesize dopamine from L-DOPA also shows marked differences among strains. For example, strains such as C57B16J (high brain amines) can synthesize far more dopamine from a given dose of L-DOPA than the ICR (low amine) strain. Because man and mouse have so many biochemical systems in common, we can perhaps be allowed to project these findings and suggest that in man wide variations in brain amines may occur and that the ability to utilize and synthesize these modulators may also vary widely. Since mild depression and mood swings are common to nearly everyone, these systems concerned with mood must be just sufficient to keep a normal balance. Stress or changes due to age and endocrine function may cause these biochemical systems to lose their ability to maintain the balance essential to normal mood swing.

It would indeed be short-sighted to think that these biogenic amines are the whole story. Their interrelation with cholinergic systems must be considered of major importance.[5] In addition, the interrelation of the biogenic amines and various endocrine systems suggests that these are essential in considering any problems of mood or brain function. The recent studies of thyroid function as related to depression support this contention,[7] as do the well-known mood swings related to the menstrual cycle.

From these various lines of thought, we can perhaps summarize our point of view on this complex problem of mood and especially depression.

Although the clinical results to date do not give a clear picture as to the relation of biogenic amines to mood, they do show that these amines are most certainly involved. However, they can only be a part of this complex problem. The interrelation with cholinergic systems needs further investigation, and, above all, the role of endocrine systems in the function of these amines will be a rich area for future research.

The clinical effectiveness of electroshock therapy in depression may be a key to this problem through study of concomitant or post-seizure changes in brain biochemistry and endocrine function. Further work in this area will undoubtedly reveal important factors in mood control.

The genetic approach to the various enzymes and systems involved in controlling the levels of biogenic amines at receptor sites will be of major importance in future research into the etiology of mental diseases, especially depression and mania. Knowledge of the interrelation of these biochemical factors with neuro-endocrine modalities will also be essential to our understanding of these complex systems, all of which are essential in determining the functional state of the nervous system. Although the model of depression as a "deficiency disease" is still a useful one, the final picture will be a complex one in which the imbalance of systems will probably give us our best understanding of and approach to the problem.

REFERENCES

1. Bunney, W. E., Jr., Brodie, H., Murphy, D. L., and Goodwin, F. K. (1971). Studies of alpha-methyl-para-tyrosine, L-DOPA and L-tryptophane in depression and mania. *American Journal of Psychiatry*, 127:872.

2. Coppen, A., Shaw, D. M., Malleson, A., Eccleston, E., and Gundy, G. (1965). Tryptophane metabolism in depression. *British Journal of Psychiatry*, 111:993.

3. Everett, G. M. (1970). Evidence for dopamine as a central neuromodulator: Neurological and behavioral implications. In: L-DOPA and Parkinsonism, edited by A. Barbeau and F. H. McDowell. Davis Co., Philadelphia, p. 364.

4. Everett, G. M., and Toman, J. E. P. (1959). Mode of action of rauwolfia alkaloids and motor activity. In: *Biological Psychiatry*, edited by J. H. Masserman. Grune and Stratton, New York. p. 75.

5. Karczmar, A. G., Nishi, S., and Blaber, L. C. (1972). Synaptic modulations in brain and human behavior. In: *Brain and Human Behavior*, edited by A. G. Karczmar and J. C. Eccles. Springer-Verlag, New York.

6. Murphy, D. L. (1971). Regular induction of hypomania by L-DOPA in bipolar manic-depressive patients. *Nature*, 229:135.

7. Prang, A. J., Jr., Wilson, I. C., Rabon, A. M., and Lipton, M. A. (1969). Enhancement of imipramine antidepressant activity by thyroid hormone. *American Journal of Psychiatry*, 126:457.

8. Schildkraut, J. J., Davis, J. M., and Klerman, G. L. (1968). Biochemistry of depressions. In: *Psychopharmacology*, edited by D. H. Efron. U.S. Govt. Printing Office, Washington.

Discussion and Conclusions

Irwin J. Kopin

The chapters in this volume are remarkable in their agreement on the major psychiatric effects of L-DOPA in both parkinsonian and depressed patients. It appears that L-DOPA produces some degree of alertness and an enhanced feeling of well-being, but no striking effect on depression. In retarded-depressed patients there appears to be some increase in motor activity, and in some depressed patients the feeling of well-being may progress to a hypomania. There is some suggestion that the hypomanic state occurs only in patients who have had previous episodes of mania and may therefore be considered to have the "bipolar" form of affective disorder, but there is not uniform agreement on this point, and it is likely that more patients will have to be studied before the validity of this association can be determined. Agitated-depressed patients and schizophrenics are not helped by L-DOPA, and it is possible that L-DOPA may worsen their condition.

The psychiatric disorders produced in parkinsonian patients are relatively infrequent, resemble toxic psychosis with confusion or delirium, and almost always occur in patients with a previous history of psychic disorder. The symptoms appear relatively soon after initiation of L-DOPA therapy, occur more frequently in elderly individuals, and regress relatively rapidly when treatment is stopped. In general, it is unusual for parkinsonian patients to develop symptoms of psychosis *de novo*.

Because of the obvious benefit parkinsonian patients derive from treatment with L-DOPA, they have received the substance for much longer intervals than have psychiatric patients. Those who use L-DOPA for treatment of parkinsonism point out that it is the length of time of treatment with adequate doses of L-DOPA, rather than the level attained, which is important to achieve maximal benefit from the medication. In some patients who have been treated unsuccessfully for over 3 months, depression may appear; however this appears to be situational rather than drug-induced.

It appears that administration of L-DOPA may be attended by effects which appear relatively soon after initiation of therapy and disappear rapidly after discontinuation of treatment; other effects appear only after a longer interval and disappear slowly. In attempting to explain the mechanisms by which L-DOPA may produce its effects, involvement of compounds with rapid turnover may account for the acute effects of the drug while other substances with a relatively slow turnover may be associated with the more chronic effects. The introduction of L-DOPA for treatment of parkinsonism stems from the observation that dopamine levels in the striatum are low in this disorder,[1] presumably as a consequence of the degeneration of the nigra-striatal dopaminergic neurons. It does not appear likely that treatment with L-DOPA restores these neurons; however, replacement of the dopamine may produce effects which restore, at least in part, the function of portions of the motor systems controlled by these neurons.

There is little doubt that treatment with L-DOPA results in formation of dopamine in brain, even after destruction of dopaminergic cells. The effects of formation of dopamine in cells which do not normally contain this amine are not well defined. Treatment with L-DOPA decreases serotonin levels in brain.[2] There is some evidence that dopamine formed in non-dopaminergic neurons may displace the amines in those cells and function as substitute "false" transmitters. The actions of dopamine derived from DOPA in these neurons might account for the rapidly appearing (and disappearing) "side effects" of L-DOPA.[3] In brain, norepinephrine formation is only slightly accelerated by L-DOPA treatment.[4] The displacement of norepinephrine by dopamine may account for the alerting effects observed. It appears that in brain, dopamine-β-hydroxylase may be almost rate limiting; in the peripheral sympathetic neurons, tyrosine hydroxylation is much slower than β-hydroxylation of dopamine.

The levels of L-DOPA which are used clinically are in the range of a food rather than a medication and are equivalent to the intake of other amino acids. These doses may produce a number of biochemical effects in addition to formation of dopamine. The acute effects of DOPA administration would be expected on biochemical processes in which there is a relatively rapid turnover of the substrates. Effects of L-DOPA which develop only slowly are more probably related to alterations of more slowly replaced substances. The relatively slow turnover of membranes (including receptors), proteins (including enzymes), and other structural components of cells makes these more likely candidates for mediating slowly developing effects than the small molecules. The metabolites of L-DOPA and dopamine include O-methylated catecholamines. Large doses of L-DOPA increase utilization of methionine, and levels of S-adenosylmethionine (SAME) are lowered.[5] Since SAME is the methyl donor for a wide variety of methyl-containing compounds, the rate of formation of these compounds may be diminished. Thus methylation of catechols, histamine, precursors of choline-containing lipids, nicotinamide, etc., may be slowed.[6] Formation of spermine and spermidine from putrescine and the decarboxylated product of SAME may also be diminished. Furthermore, utilization of methionine for methylation might interfere with availability of this essential amino acid for protein synthesis.

The extent to which L-DOPA or its O-methylated derivative, 3-methoxytyrosine, might interfere with amino acid transport or replace amino acids normally used in protein synthesis is unknown. The presence of large amounts of DOPA, which diminishes the need for tyrosine hydroxylation, may result in decreased levels of tyrosine hydroxylase. The accumulation of dopamine might induce formation of more dopamine-β-hydroxylase. There may also be changes in levels of the enzymes which metabolize the catecholamines (catechol-O-methyltransferase and monoamine oxidase). Thus there are a number of possible mechanisms by which chronic treatment with L-DOPA may alter protein synthesis, membrane formation, enzyme levels, etc. These biochemical changes would be relatively slow; their effects may not become manifest for some time and would be expected to persist for a period after cessation of treatment.

REFERENCES

1. Birkmeyer, W., and Hornykiewicz, O. (1961). *Wein. Klin. Wschr.,* 73:787.

2. Bartholini, G., de Prada, M., and Pletscher, A. (1968). *J. Pharm. Pharmacol.,* 20:228.

3. Ng, K. Y., Chase, T. N., Colburn, R. W., and Kopin, I. J. (1970). *Science,* 170:76.

4. Everetts, G. M., and Borcherding, J. W. (1970). *Science,* 168:849.

5. Wurtman, R. J., Rose, C. M., Matthysse, S., Stephenson, J., and Baldessarini, R. (1970). *Science,* 169:395.

6. Thoa, N. B., Weise, V. K., and Kopin, I. J. *Biochem. Pharm. (in press).*

Index

INDEX

DOPA,
abnormal metabolites of, 21
alerting effect, 11, 59, 137
antagonism of reserpine-induced parkinsonism, 125
catatonia, induction of, 17, 18
cognitive functions, effects on, 23–24
depression, therapy of, 81–84, 87–100, 103–118, 132
disturbed sensory perception, induction of, 18
disturbed thought content, induction of, 17, 93
effect on brain catecholamine levels, 98, 99, 139
effect on akinesia in Parkinson's disease, 12, 13, 14
effect on brain serotonin levels, 99
effect on S-adenosylmethionine in brain, 99, 140
effect on schizophrenic patients, 123–126
effect on turnover of noradrenaline, 12
hypomania, induction of, 17, 93–95, 132, 137
impotence, treatment of, 73–79
insomnia, induction of, 17
manic-depressive syndromes, therapy of, 95–98
metabolism of, 89, 98
paranoia, induction of, 17
peripheral DOPA decarboxylase inhibitors in conjunction with, 89
protein synthesis, effects on, 20
psychiatric side effects of, 16–20, 57–71, 93, 122
psychomotor activation, 93
reversal of depression in Parkinson's disease, 11, 69
reversal of drug-induced depression, 10, 131
sexual activity, effects on, 60
similarity of L-DOPA-induced behavioral abnormalities to those of amphetamine, 68
stereotyped behavior, induction of, 17
Dopamine, 15, 132
autonomic and endocrine modulation, 9

correlation between brain levels and behavior, 78
deficiency in Parkinson's disease, 9
distribution in brain, 9
dopaminergic component of amphetamine-induced stereotyped gnawing in rat, 51
effect on turnover rate caused by butyrophenones and phenothiazines, 19
role in Gilles de la Tourette syndrome, 14
role in mood regulation, 12, 83, 87
stress, effects on turnover rate of, 22
striatal activation of turnover rate of, 22
uptake into corpus striatum, 36–47
Dopamine-β-hydroxylase, 84, 139, 140
Doxepin, 46
Dreaming, effect of L-DOPA on, 17, 60
Dyskinesia, 123

Electro-shock therapy of depression, 115

"False" transmitters, 139

Gamma-aminobutyric acid, 20, 99
Gilles de la Tourette syndrome, 14

Haloperidol, 125
Homovanillic acid, 19
Hypomanic behavior, induction of by L-DOPA, 16, 17, 62, 137

Imipramine, 45, 46, 115
Impotence, effect of L-DOPA on, 73–79
Iproniazid, 131
Isocarboxazid, 51

Libido increase after L-DOPA administration in Parkinson's disease, 69
Lithium carbonate, 15

Mania, 20, 137
dopamine excretion in, 16
possible excess of brain amines in, 15
lithium therapy of, 15
Manic-depressive psychosis, 16, 63
3-Methoxytyrosine, 140

INDEX

α-Methyl-DOPA-hydrazine (MK 485), 89
Monoamine oxidase inhibitors, 35, 36, 51
  blockade of catecholamine uptake, 52
  decreased rate of monoamine
    metabolism, 11
  side effects of, 53

Nialamide, 51
Nicotinic acid, 126
Noradrenaline, 10, 12, 13, 15, 20, 132
  correlation between brain levels and
    behavior, 78
  effect of L-DOPA on rate of turnover, 12
  role in mood regulation, 12, 13, 83
  uptake into synaptosomes of corpus
    striatum, 36–40
Nortriptyline, 45, 46

Pargyline, 51
Parkinson's disease
  akinesia, 12, 81
  amphetamine and, 41
  behavioral abnormalities in patients re-
    ceiving L-DOPA, 61–71, 122
  benztropine and, 41
  dopamine deficiency in, 9
  increase in sexual activity in patients
    receiving L-DOPA, 73
  L-DOPA reversal of depression, 11, 69,
    131
  lithium therapy of manic reactions to
    L-DOPA, 16
  reversal of reserpine-induced
    parkinsonism, 125

rigidity, 12, 81
  trihexyphenidyl and, 41
Parnate, (see tranylcypromine, 36)
Phenelzine, 51, 121
Phenothiazines, 19
Phenylcyclopropylamine, 53
Protriptyline, 45, 46

Reserpine, 77
Reserpine-induced depression, 10, 131
Ro 4–4602, 77

S-adenosylmethionine, 21, 140
  effects of L-DOPA on, 20
Schizophrenia, 69
  L-DOPA effects on patients, 122–123
Scopolamine, 42, 44
Serotonin, 11, 15, 20, 132
  effect of L-DOPA on brain levels of, 99
  role in mood regulation, 13
Sexual activity, effect of L-DOPA on, 60,
  73–79, 123–126
Striatum, 9, 22–24, 39, 52
Substantia nigra, 9

Thyroid function as related to depression,
  133
Tricyclic anti-depressants, 117
  inhibition of catecholamine uptake, 11,
    36, 41, 43, 45
  mode of action, 52
Trihexyphenidyl, 41
Tyrosine-hydroxylase, 84, 139